I'm a Busybody

I'm a Busybody

CARL GLICK

Thomas Y. Crowell Company

NEW YORK

.G4 9⁶5A

Typography by George Nehrbas

Manufactured in the United States of America by the
Vail-Ballou Press, Inc., Binghamton, New York

To
Marion

Contents

I'm a Busybody

1

SAINTS AND SINNERS

ONE summer the family took a trip to California. I was fourteen at the time, was wearing my first pair of long trousers, and felt very grown up. So did my spindly-legged sister. She had some new dresses, had taken her hair out of pigtails, and had it wound high on her head in the approved style of the day. Someone had foolishly told her that this made her look like a Gibson girl. So whenever I tried to talk with her, she would turn her head away, and all I could see was the fashionable Gibson profile. This annoyed me.

Mother had a couple of new hats, which she carried in two paper hat boxes. They were always getting in the way, and mother worried all summer lest I sit on the boxes or put my feet through them. Father was quite content. He had a whole box of cigars that his business partner had given him.

We took the Canadian Pacific out of Minneapolis. It was early in June and travel was light. The only other persons in our Pullman were two well-dressed elderly ladies. They seemed friendly, so it didn't take us long to get acquainted. One lady I liked especially well. She reminded me of my Sunday School teacher, and I told her so. This pleased her. She said that back in her Massachusetts town she was Secretary of the Christian Endeavor Society and an active member of the Woman's Christian Temperance Union.

I told her that I thought drink was a terrible curse, as it ruined not only a man's health but his pocketbook as well. She said she thought I was a very sweet and moral young man with high ideals. Thus encouraged, I told her all about myself—about my pony Billy, about my Aunt Rachel, a maiden lady of unsettled years who lived with us, and who played the organ in our church, about my friends back home in Marshalltown, Iowa, and how we gave shows for pins in the backyard. I told her I liked to read books and play the piano.

She asked me what I was going to be when I grew up. I said that Father wanted me to go into business with him. He was a manufacturer of gasoline engines and furnaces. But I didn't like that, as I thought machines were uninteresting. Mother wanted me to be a newspaper editor, and then in time become Ambassador to England. That, I felt, would be a lot more fun than being a manufacturer, as I would get to meet and know a lot of people, and maybe even someday write a book about them. My new-found friend agreed with me. She was most kind and sympathetic, and I decided she was one of the nicest persons I had ever met.

We were crossing the dreary plains of Canada, mile after mile as flat as the top of a table. Now and then we'd whizz past a farmhouse and a barn. Sometimes there'd be a lone tree by the house. But more often not—just the lonely house and the stark barn.

"What desolate country," I said. "This would be a perfect spot in which to expiate a murder!"

But somehow my words of wisdom and my astute observation didn't impress my lady friend. She suddenly became silent. Conversation between us ended with a dull thump.

After an awkward pause, I stammered lamely, "It's been nice meeting you—but I guess I'd better go back to my seat."

"Yes—do," she said abruptly.

Of course I immediately told my mother of this conversation. She couldn't understand what I had said that was wrong. She fully agreed with me that we were passing through desolate country and it would be a fine spot in which to expiate a murder.

When the charming lady with whom I had been talking went in to the dining car for lunch, Mother saw on her seat a book she had been reading. Now Mother, being a nosy and snoopy person, as I am, picked up the book and glanced quickly at the flyleaf. She looked a trifle pale when she came back to our seat.

"You certainly did say the wrong thing, Carl," she said. "Where's your father? I want to speak with him."

"Why?" I asked. "He's in the smoking car."

"Because," said Mother grimly, "the lady's name—if she is a lady—is on the flyleaf. She's Lizzie Borden."

"Who's she?" I asked.

"A notorious murderess!" exclaimed Mother. "There's a poem about her that goes like this:

> *Lizzie Borden took an ax*
> *And gave her mother forty whacks.*
> *When she saw what she had done,*
> *She gave her father forty-one!"*

Mother went on to tell me that, only a few years previously, Lizzie Borden had been arrested and tried for murdering both her mother and her stepfather. She had been accused of braining them with a hatchet. However, she was acquitted, although in Fall River, Massachusetts, where the deed was done, there were two schools of thought as to her guilt. Still, on her stepfather's death, she and her sister inherited $175,000.

"No wonder she can afford to dress well and travel in Pullmans," said Mother.

"So do we," I suggested.

"It's quite different with us," said Mother, haughtily.

But Mother was really frightened, and she didn't like the idea of traveling halfway across the continent with a murderess.

"Not in a half-empty Pullman where I can't even lock the curtains of my berth," Mother exclaimed. "Please tell your father to come here immediately."

Mother persuaded Father to ask the conductor if we couldn't stop over at the next station. Father meekly arranged it. So we spent the night and part of the next day at a small, wild frontier town, which turned out to be exciting for me. On the main street were Indians, mounted policemen, and cowboys. I'd never seen a cowboy before. Mother was quite happy, too. She put on her best hat and went shopping. But she didn't buy anything. She just wanted to compare the prices in Canada with those in Iowa.

Father's only comment was, "Be careful what you say to strangers, Carl. Never discuss politics or religion. Both lead to murder."

I suppose I should have learned a lesson from this and taken Father's advice. But I didn't. I've been talking to strangers all my life. And why not? I'm a writer, and curious about people. If I didn't get to know and understand people, what would I write about? The birds, the bees, and the flowers?

I've found, after the opening conversational shots are fired— something about the weather is always good—that I can learn a lot if I say innocently, "I'm a writer."

Invariably the stranger will smile sadly and remark, "I had something happen to me once that I always thought would make a good story."

We're off! I've met some people who have told me the most

intimate details of their lives. I've heard things about them that they wouldn't dream of confiding to their best friends, or even to a priest at confessional. They find it easy to lay bare their souls to a stranger. They'll probably never see him again, so they confess all. I've heard a lot of fascinating off-the-record stories. Some I've used. Others I've thought had best be quickly forgotten.

So on the drop of a hat, and with or without the slightest provocation, I'll start a conversation with a stranger. Sue, my wife, thinks it's a bad habit.

"Someday you're going to say something to a stranger and he'll hit you," she has warned.

One hot summer night not so long ago we were walking along Bank Street in Greenwich Village. It's a very respectable block with some high-priced apartments. A man came out of a snooty-looking house, clad in pajamas, a bathrobe, and slippers. He aroused my curiosity. Where was he going and why?

As he came up I asked casually, "Fire?"

He drew back, angrier than a trapped tomcat.

"You're going to get hit!" murmured Sue softly. "I told you so! You're going to get hit!"

I thought so, too. This was it—and I deserved it. So I just stood there and smiled wanly.

He glared at me a moment, then snapped, "Yes—damn it! Fire! Fire! Fire!"

Then he strode down the street. I was disappointed. I never did find out why he was walking down the street in his pajamas.

Besides mentioning the weather or asking an impersonal question, there are several ways of starting a conversation. One, which I don't recommend highly, is what I call the direct approach. Now

I pride myself on my powers of observation. I fancy that I can sometimes tell a person's occupation merely by looking at him. Most people engaged in a trade or profession sooner or later take on habits and characteristics peculiar to their occupation. Doctors, for instance, even in private conversation seem to have a friendly, "cheer up, you'll be all right in a few days," soft-spoken bedside manner. Schoolteachers, neatly but plainly dressed, have an eager "tell me more" and "I want to know about you too" look. Society dowagers are usually plump, with large bosoms and costume jewelry, and have a fragrance all their own. And so on.

The great master at this business of merely glancing at people and telling them all about themselves was, of course, Sherlock Holmes. His powers of deduction were extraordinary.

He once said to a lady, "You have come by train this morning, I see. . . . I observe the second half of a return ticket in the palm of your left glove. . . . You had a good drive in a dogcart, along heavy roads before you reached the station. . . . The left arm of your jacket is spattered with mud in no less than seven places."

Wonderful! I've fancied that I have some of the same powers of acute deduction as Sherlock Holmes. Once in a dining car, facing me across the table, was a silent, gloomy chap. I started a conversation by mumbling something about the weather. No answer.

I made a comment about the scenery. He merely grunted and replied, "Yes, it's nice."

There was only one thing to do—give him the shock treatment. So I said, "I gather you are a doctor."

"I'm not a doctor," he mumbled, and continued eating his dinner.

I thought I'd try again. "Maybe you're a college professor?"

"Why do you think I'm a college professor?" he snapped.

I went on as Sherlock Holmes would have done, saying, "You seem lost in thought, intent on some academic problem."

"I'm not a college professor," he said bluntly.

I couldn't stop guessing now, so I murmured somewhat weakly, "Certainly you're a professional man of some sort."

"Now, why?"

"Your hands. They're not the hands of a laborer. And you're obviously not a salesman because—"

"Because why?"

"You haven't tried to sell me anything."

He made no comment, but went on with his dinner. It was time for me to confess. "I'm a writer," I said.

He didn't seem the least bit interested.

"I try to observe people," I boasted. "I try to make deductions and find out about them—just like Sherlock Holmes."

"You do, do you?" he said, giving me a sharp glance. And then he smiled as he added, "Since you're so damned curious, I'll tell you who I am. I'm a member of the FBI—and here's my badge to prove it. Better luck next time in your deductions, Sherlock!"

Then there's another very good approach. That is to tell the stranger all about yourself. That may get him interested and then he'll talk. My Aunt Rachel once used this method in talking to a stranger, with results that were both unexpected and startling. Aunt Rachel was a model of propriety, a good and virtuous woman. She taught a class in Sunday School, played the organ in the church, and was an active and earnest worker in the Ladies' Aid Society. She disapproved of card playing and smoking, and often

boasted that "Lips that touch liquor shall never touch mine."
Then one summer she went to California to visit her sister, my
Aunt Mina.

"Be careful and watch your step," I cautioned Aunt Rachel as
she boarded the train. "Don't get into trouble."

"Please don't say things like that, Carl," she replied. "You know
I've never been in trouble in all my life!"

At Stockton she changed from the transcontinental train to the
day coach that was to take her to Tuolumne, a small mining and
lumber town in the mountains, where Aunt Mina lived. Seated
next to Aunt Rachel was a charming lady. Of course they got
to talking. The lady was going to Tuolumne, too. Aunt Rachel
asked her if she knew her sister, Mrs. Bartlett.

"I don't know her personally," replied the lady, "but I know
who she is."

Then Aunt Rachel told this lady the story of her life, and
showed her snapshots to prove it. The lady was interested and very
friendly. Aunt Rachel took a great fancy to her.

"You must come and see me, my dear," said Aunt Rachel.

"Thank you. I'd love to," responded the lady.

When Aunt Rachel got off the train, she was hoping to introduce
her new-found friend to Aunt Mina, but the lady somehow vanished in the crowd. When Aunt Rachel described the lady to Aunt
Mina, Aunt Mina couldn't place her. Aunt Rachel realized that
she hadn't learned the lady's name. Of course Aunt Mina gave
tea parties for Aunt Rachel and introduced her to all her friends.
But the lady on the train was never among them.

Then one day Aunt Rachel was shopping with Aunt Mina.
There in the store was her friend.

"My dear, my dear!" cried Aunt Rachel, with her usual Christian friendliness. Rushing up to the lady, she kissed her on both cheeks. "Why haven't you been to see me?"

The clerks gasped. Aunt Mina gulped. A chilled silence greeted Aunt Rachel's enthusiasm.

"I've been very, very busy," the lady responded politely.

Aunt Rachel was on the point of introducing her friend to Aunt Mina, but Aunt Mina suddenly found something to interest her several counters away. The new-found friend slipped out of Aunt Rachel's clutches and departed from the store.

Later Aunt Mina told Aunt Rachel the truth. Her friend was the madame of the town's one notorious bawdy house.

"Well," said Aunt Rachel bravely, "I don't care! She may not go to church every Sunday as I do—but I found her interesting!"

Of course, what Aunt Rachel discovered is quite true. Often sinners can be very interesting. They can be very dull, too. And the same can be said of saints. It's sometimes hard to tell the difference. One person behaves in a certain fashion and it's all wrong. Someone else may do exactly the same thing and it's perfectly all right. So few, very few people are examples of a perfect saint. And very few are really hardened criminals. There's a little of the saint and the sinner in all of us. It's the combination of good and evil in the people I know, I find, that makes them interesting.

I once met a Hindu mystic who was so holy he hadn't spoken for fifteen years. Yet the manner in which he inveigled money for his support from society dowagers had all the earmarks of a first-class swindle. Nor was he too unlike a panhandler I met one noon when I was living in New York on Madison Avenue.

He was a shabbily dressed, middle-aged man, and I smelt liquor on his breath as he asked me for a dime for a cup of coffee.

I smiled sadly as I said, "I haven't had anything to eat myself today." (Quite true. I had just gotten up.)

"Tough," he murmured.

"I don't know where or how I'll have lunch—if I have lunch." (Again true, for breakfast would keep me going until dinner time.)

"Too bad," he said.

"I'm having to move next week. I won't be able to pay the rent where I'm staying." (Also true, as I was leaving town for the winter, to direct a Little Theater in Florida.)

"You giving me this straight?" he asked.

I nodded, and sighed even more sadly. I never feel too bright, anyway, in the morning before breakfast.

"Come with me," he said. "I'll stake you to a cup of coffee."

He led me to the Automat, bought me coffee and a roll—and I let him. He confessed that he made ten to fifteen dollars a day panhandling, and had some twelve dollars on him at the moment —which, incidentally, was more cash than I had in my pocket.

"Look," he said. "Why don't you try panhandling. That damned sad smile you got ought to work it easy. I'll show you all the tricks, and you give me ten percent of your first week's earnings. Is it a deal?"

Since I already had a literary agent, I didn't feel like taking on any more obligations at the moment. I told him I'd have to think it over.

But he went on and told me a lot of things I didn't know about panhandlers and their methods. Later I used this informa- tion in a mystery novel and, remembering this man, put him into the book and entitled one of the chapters "The Panhandler with a Tuxedo." Had I known where to find him, I would have sent him a copy autographed "Yours gratefully." But probably that would have been an unnecessary gesture on my part, for he could well afford to buy the book himself.

I've found it isn't only from strangers that material for stories can be obtained. Any writer, if he really makes the effort to become acquainted with his own family, does a bit of sleuthing at home, and has no hesitancy in reading grandmother's love letters (especially if they weren't written by grandfather), will have plenty of sources for yarns.

I know that's been true of me. Once my sister said she shuddered and had nervous indigestion every time she saw one of my stories in print, because she dreaded to discover what episode in our private family fortunes I'd be telling next. There was one aunt in particular who, being somewhat unconventional, gave me inspiration in more ways than one.

2

AMERICA—'TIS OF THEE

In 1943 I took a trip to California. My train passed through Marshalltown, Iowa, where I was born. I wanted to stop off, as it had been nearly thirty years since I had paid a visit to my old home town. But I was told that if I did, there was no guarantee (since there was a war on) that I could get a reservation for the rest of my journey.

As the train sped past the town, I stood on the back platform and saw once again the old familiar landmarks: the Court House rising above the green trees, Varnum's Hill, where I used to go coasting in winter, and the woods outside the town, where we'd picked wild flowers in the spring. Tears came to my eyes. A gruff, hard-boiled army sergeant standing beside me stared.

"Got something in your eye, pal?" he asked.

"No," I replied. "This is the town where I was born, where I went to school, where five generations of my family lie at rest in the cemetery. I can't stop off—and if I want to shed a tear or two, thinking of the good old days, that's my own damn business. To hell with you!"

"I know how you feel, pal," he said sympathetically. "If I went back to my home town, they'd arrest me, too. Here—" and he pulled a pint of whisky from his pocket—"have a snort. You'll feel better."

But my thoughts were in the past, recalling my rebellious boyhood days and my breaking away from the conventional ties that bound me; and as I lifted the bottle to my lips, I said, "Here's to America—thank God for her!"

"Amen!" said the sergeant, taking a snort. "The land of the free and the home of the brave."

"Quite true," I echoed. "Just like her. She always thought so, too."

"*She?* Who's *she?*" asked the sergeant, puzzled.

I thought I had better explain. "When I made that toast, I was thinking of another America."

"What other America is there?" snapped the sergeant.

"My Aunt America."

"Sure—I get you," grinned the sergeant. "That calls for another snort. Here's to her husband, Uncle Sam!"

"But his name wasn't Sam," I said. "It was Cliff."

"What in hell are you talking about?" asked the sergeant, giving me a peculiar look.

"It's this way," I said, patiently. "When I was a lad, I had an aunt named Emma."

"Yeah?" said the sergeant. "I'm listening."

"Well, she didn't like the name Emma, so she insisted on being called America. When I once asked her why, she said, 'Isn't America the land of the free and the home of the brave? I'm both, and I intend to live up to my name, bigawd.' And she did, too, and she helped me sign my Declaration of Independence. She was the first rebel I'd ever met, the first person to give me a glimpse of what might be an exciting and interesting world beyond the hills that surrounded Marshalltown.—Does this make sense?"

"No," said the sergeant.

I reached for the bottle, as I felt I needed another drink. "Aunt America liked to drink out of a bottle, too," I said.

But the sergeant snapped on the cork and thrust the bottle back into his pocket.

"You've had enough," he said, not too ungraciously. "Relax, pal. Take it easy. And you'd better be going back into the car. You might fall off the platform."

"Thanks for the drinks—and the good advice," I said meekly.

As I walked away, I saw him shaking his head sadly and heard him mutter, "It takes all kinds to make a world."

By the time I found my seat, Marshalltown had vanished in the distance, and the train was speeding through the green, rolling prairies of Iowa. But my thoughts went back to over forty years ago, and I recalled the Marshalltown I had known as a boy—and Aunt America.

Back home when a man reached the age of thirty-plus and hadn't married, people would frown and say to him, "Tch! Tch! Remember poor Cliff Will? He waited until he was your age before he married—and look what happened to him!"

Now Uncle Cliff was one of my favorite uncles. He was a partner in the McBride and Will Drug Store on the corner of Main Street across from the Court House. It was a wonderful store—had everything a drugstore should have, mysterious medicines in fancy-colored bottles, and a soda fountain.

Uncle Cliff possessed a genial manner and a booming laugh, and whenever some of my friends and myself would troop into the drugstore and line up at the fountain, he'd say, "How are you, men? What's the drink today?" Just as if we were really grown up and standing with our right foot on the rail at the bar of the saloon down the block—forbidden territory to us.

Now and then I heard vague rumors about him, but that never bothered me. His friendliness and the respect he paid me proved that Uncle Cliff could do no wrong. However, rumor had it that he took a drink now and then, and also that his frequent trips to Chicago were not wholly devoted to business.

It was on one of these so-called business trips that the awful thing happened. He got married, most unexpectedly and without any previous notice or warning. It was a great surprise to everyone when Cliff came home with his bride. The relatives all sighed with relief. Now, they felt, Cliff would settle down and raise a family, which was what everybody else did in those days.

But his wife wasn't the domestic sort. At first she didn't even want to live at the Will home. She preferred a suite of rooms at the hotel. Such a thing was unheard of. In those days hotels were only for traveling men. Up went the eyebrows. And then the rumors started.

Aunt America was the type of woman who invariably invites gossip. Had she been dumpy, plain, and unassuming, probably no one would have murmured. But she wasn't. She was one of the most beautiful women who ever came to Marshalltown as a blushing bride. She used rouge in a day when respectable ladies didn't paint their faces like professional hussies. Even while dining at the hotel she'd have a highball brought to her table—and drink it, too, right in public, where everybody could see her. In those days good women didn't even have a cocktail at home.

Of course people talked. One of our neighbors in particular was

an awful gossip. Mother, behind her back, had nicknamed her
"Mrs. Snoopy." She came to see Mother one afternoon. Mother
told us about their conversation at supper that night.

"How she learns all these things is beyond me," said Mother.
"She knows more about our private affairs and the family business
than I do. She thinks she pumps me. Well, I just let her think so."

Mother was pretty good at pumping people herself. She could
sit quietly mending socks and appear much more interested in the
mending than the conversation, as she would ask the most seemingly innocent questions. When Mrs. Snoopy came in that afternoon, Mother plumped her down in the rocking chair and went
right on mending.

"I hear Cliff Will married a widow," said Mrs. Snoopy. "Is
she grass or sod?"

"Sod," said Mother.

"I heard she was grass."

"Sod!" said Mother with a tone of finality. And when Mother
made a statement that was final, it was final, and no more questions asked. "Her first husband was a policeman, I've been told,
and was shot."

"Hm," said Mrs. Snoopy. "By whom?"

"How do I know?" said Mother. "I wasn't there—and I've the
decency not to ask."

But that didn't stop Mrs. Snoopy. "I hear, too, she's a foreigner."

"Aren't we all?" replied Mother. "My husband's family came
from Germany, and mine from Ireland. Where did your family
come from?"

"England."

"Well, I guess that makes you a foreigner, too," replied Mother.

"But I hear she's a real foreigner—has Spanish blood in her.

And she just calls herself America to cover up. Why, if she is an American, doesn't she use an American name?"

But Mother had an answer for that one, as she said, "The only real American names I know are Sitting Bull and Rain-in-the-Face."

Mrs. Snoopy had other questions. "Where did Cliff meet her?"

"In Chicago."

"But just where in Chicago?" leered Mrs. Snoopy. "That's the point!"

"Why don't you ask Cliff?"

"I did—and he said the same thing you said, 'In Chicago!' That sort of makes me wonder."

"Just exactly what are you trying to insinuate?" asked Mother.

"Well—I heard Cliff didn't have to marry her if he didn't want to."

Mother kept right on with her mending. "I'm glad I haven't a nasty mind," she said sweetly.

"Neither have I," snapped back Mrs. Snoopy. "And there are no merry widows in our family, either!"

Mother was silent. After a long, embarrassing pause Mrs. Snoopy rose. "Well—I guess I'd better be going back home."

"Thanks for telling me all those things about dear Cliff's wife," said Mother. "Have you any more questions?"

"Yes," said Mrs. Snoopy, eagerly. "What is the family going to do—and how are they going to treat her?"

"Exactly as the wife of Cousin Cliff should be treated—with proper respect, as becomes a bride. We shall all entertain her."

And they did. While some of my other aunts didn't quite approve of Aunt America, still they felt that they were the only ones privileged to criticize her. Should anyone else make a comment about a member of the clan—them was fighting words, pardner! So to the town the family presented a united front, kept a stiff upper lip, and gave formal dinner parties to welcome Aunt America to Marshalltown.

At the first few dinners Aunt America was very well behaved. She merely sat quietly and looked over the relatives carefully and let them do the talking. It was customary in those days, after dinner, for the men to remain seated around the table, having a nip of port and smoking cigars. Cigarettes were taboo. It was only poolroom loafers who used what were called "coffin nails." And no woman even dreamed of smoking.

The ladies, leaving the men folk to their stories, would retire to the parlor and there, over the coffee cups, gossip to their heart's content. Aunt America always looked a trifle dazed as she listened to the usual run of small talk: how to take care of babies properly, the price of eggs, what bargains were to be had at the stores, and all those everyday problems so dear to the hearts of housewives.

But finally the day came when Aunt America couldn't stand it any longer. It was at the dinner party given for her and Uncle Cliff by Aunt Anna and Uncle Larry. The dessert had been served and eaten. Aunt Anna rose and said as usual to the ladies, "Shall we retire to the parlor?"

Up bobbed the ladies. But Aunt America remained seated.

"No, thanks," she said sweetly. "You girls go along. I'll stay here with the men and have a cigarette. I think I've a couple of stories about traveling salesman they will enjoy, too!"

It was a breath-taking moment. And a dead silence greeted Aunt America's unconventional behavior. Even the men gasped.

But Aunt Anna faced the situation bravely, and as a proper

hostess said graciously, "Yes, do, please. Perhaps you boys will tell us the stories later."

The ladies retired to the parlor. It was a tense moment, as they sat and listened to the roars of laughter that came from the dining room. Aunt America could tell a story with gusto and bring out all the varied shades of meaning. And she did smoke a cigarette. It was the first time a woman had ever smoked a cigarette in Marshalltown.

When the port was passed around in the dining room, Aunt America poured herself a large glass and said to the men, "I usually like my liquor straight out of the bottle, but tonight I'm being a lady."

Then she said, "It's a fine town you've got here, boys. It's law-abiding, and that makes things easy for me. When your kids misbehave, you spank them, feed 'em castor oil, and send 'em to bed. That's the way to treat kids. I guess I wasn't spanked enough when I was young—but there's nothing I can do about that now. I like it here. It's a fine town. But there's one thing I don't like. You've got an awful lot of old snoopies around. They've been gossiping about me, and saying all sorts of things. Well, I've had one ear to the ground, too. And I've heard a number of stories about some of you boys that won't bear repeating. So my motto is, 'Live and let live.' What do you say?"

There was one rumor, however, that annoyed her. When she heard that it was being said that she and Cliff weren't even married, she said, "I know damn well how to fix that!"

So, two months after she was married, she bought a wedding gown, the most expensive she could find. She had her picture taken in it and showed it all over town, saying, "Don't I look swell in white? Just like a virgin."

I had heard so much gossip about Aunt America that my curiosity concerning her was fairly eating me up. She obviously was so different from my other aunts, who called me "Carlie" and were always admonishing me to be a good boy, wash behind the ears, study hard, say my prayers nightly, and who told me that, if I did all those things, when I grew up I might possibly amount to something. I had met Aunt America casually, of course. However, I wanted to know her personally and talk with her. She didn't pay much attention to us youngsters. I guess she thought we were too young. But one day I had an idea.

My English teacher at high school, Miss Hathaway, assigned us as a topic for a theme, "An Interesting Person I Have Met." And who would be better to write about than Aunt America? That meant that I'd have to go and call on her and get material for my theme at first hand. I told Mother what I was planning to do.

"How will you go about it?" she asked.

"I'll just ask her a lot of questions about herself," I replied.

Mother groaned. "You're just as bad as Mrs. Snoopy—you're an old busybody," she said.

"No, I'm not," I answered. "Mrs. Snoopy gossips and butts into other people's business."

"What are you doing?" asked Mother.

"My interest is legitimate. I want to learn. And how can I write a theme about her if I don't know her personally?"

"It's all right, I suppose," said Mother. "But don't be too curious, and don't ask her a lot of silly questions about herself. Just behave properly and let her do the talking. She'll tell you a lot more if she doesn't think you're trying to pump her."

I jumped on my pony and rode into the country and gathered

a large armful of wild flowers. I thought it would be nice if I took Aunt America something.

When I rapped on the door, Aunt America opened it cautiously. I don't know what she thought, seeing me standing there, holding a big bunch of bluebells and Dutchman's-breeches.

"If it isn't one of the Dutch cousins," she said. (That's what she called the family, to their annoyance. But they weren't above reminding her of *her* Spanish blood.)

"Yes, ma'am," I said. "And I've brought you a bouquet."

"How sweet!" she exclaimed, really pleased. "I've had posies from all sorts of men, but this is the first time a kid has ever brought me wild flowers. Come in and take the rocking chair."

I was quite awed, and somewhat thrilled. I sat down, while she put the flowers in a vase.

"I love bluebells," she said. "But what are these white flowers?"

"Dutchman's-breeches, ma'am," I said.

"Migawd— In Iowa they have them on flowers, too!"

I didn't quite know how to start the conversation. And I think she was a little at a loss, also, not knowing exactly how she could entertain this gangling eighteen-year-old nephew. So she did the obvious.

Pulling out a cigarette, she asked me, "Do you smoke?"

"No, ma'am, not yet," I replied. "Father has promised me a gold watch if I don't smoke until I'm twenty-one. And I'd rather have a gold watch in three years than stunt my growth now."

"You've got the right idea," she said soberly. "Do you drink?"

"Only Peruna," I answered.

"Migawd—what's that?"

So I told her about my Grandmother Cannon, Mother's mother,

who lived with us—a gentle, lovable, quiet old lady who, being a Quaker, said "thee" and "thou." She was very fond of a patent medicine, Peruna, which contained, I suspect, a high alcoholic content. If you returned five empty bottles to the store, a sixth bottle would be given you free. It was a great day for Grandmother when she received that free bottle. So, to hasten that happy event, she shared her nightcap with me. Before going to bed nights, my Quaker Grandmother would say to me, "Thee is a growing boy, Carl. Thee isn't strong. Thou should have a little of my medicine."

When Mother discovered this, she disapproved strongly. She didn't mind Grandmother having her nightly nip, but she didn't think I should. She tried to stop Grandmother. But Grandmother, anticipating that sixth free bottle, managed to hide a small glass of Peruna in my room nights, and so I continued the drinking habit without Mother ever knowing about it.

But as I said to Aunt America, "It isn't like drinking whisky. Peruna is a sort of medicine, really. And I don't think it hurts me, do you?"

"Hell, no!" exclaimed Aunt America emphatically. "I'd offer you a real drink—but if I did, some old snoopy would be certain to find out, and I'd be talked about even more than I am now."

"Yes, ma'am," I said. "I know."

"Know what?" Her handsome eyes flashed.

This embarrassed me, for I felt I had said the wrong thing, and all I wanted was to get her talking, hoping she'd tell me the truth. So I said rather lamely, "I've heard a few things, nothing important, but I don't think they are true."

"Put it in your pipe and smoke it—they are!" she said. "But this is how I feel about it. No matter what you do, people are going to talk.

So if you want to do something in this wide, beautiful world—do it! And to hell with 'em. But remember this, for whatever you do, you always pay a price. I don't mean in dollars and cents. But there's a price on everything you do and everything you get—and if you're willing to pay that price, go ahead."

"I don't quite understand," I said—and I didn't quite, at that time.

"If you want a home and security, the price is losing some of your freedom. Part of it, at least—not all. Look at me. . . . If you want fame, and get it—you're public property; and if you don't behave, you get roasted much more than Mr. Average Citizen. If the Almighty Dollar is your god—you're liable to end up being a slave to money. There's no escape—no matter what you do. Me—I believe in doing as I damn well please. And, knowing my chin is stuck out, I'll take the socks I get with a grin. I'll mind my own damn business, too; for the other fellow's got just as much right to life, liberty, and the pursuit of happiness as I have. Let him have it, too. It won't hurt you any. . . . Well—that's the end of this sermon."

"Thanks," I said. "Just what I wanted to know. Do you mind if I quote you?"

"Quote me? Where?" she asked suspiciously.

So I told her about the theme I was going to write.

"Okay with me," she said, smiling, and then as an afterthought, "but maybe you'd better not use my name. Some of the old cats in town think I'm flirting with their husbands—God forbid! And if you came out and said I said those things, they might accuse me of corrupting youth. And that's one thing I've never done—rob the cradle."

So I wrote the theme, and my teacher gave me a good mark and said that the philosophy I expressed was very wholesome indeed. So if today I am somewhat indifferent to outworn and outmoded social conventions, and free perhaps of intolerance toward my less wayward brothers and sisters, it is due to the example Aunt America set me. Years later, when I became acquainted with the Chinese, I found that they had somewhat the same philosophy as Aunt America: a belief in the enjoyment of living, a live-and-let-live tolerance of others, and a willingness to accept the bitter with the sweet in their fellow men, with not too many questions asked. I think, had my Chinese friends known Aunt America, they would have understood and loved her, too.

After that first visit to Aunt America I would now and then, on my way home from school, drop in for a few moments' chat with her. And of course one day she asked the inevitable question every curious adult asks a youngster, "What are you going to be when you grow up —a circus clown or a policeman?"

"Neither," I answered.

"But I thought every boy had those ambitions."

"I did once," I confessed. "I thought I'd join the circus when I was eleven, and I seriously considered being a policeman when I was twelve. But now that I'm older and have more sense, I think I'll combine the two and be a writer."

"That's a new one on me—a writer," she said. "Now, why?"

"Because, being a writer, I can travel around, and from what I've read of writers, nobody cares how silly they act, like circus clowns. And since, if I write about people I've got to know about people, I can behave like a policeman—ask them a lot of questions and butt into their business."

"I get it," she said. "Sort of a professional busybody. What are you going to write?"

"I'm sort of stage-struck," I answered. "And I've just had a play published in our high school magazine which mother thinks is pretty good, so I guess I'll be a playwright."

She was interested in knowing how I would go about it, and suggested that if I wanted to be a playwright I should first of all learn something about the theater. And she thought the best way to do that was to become an actor.

"I've kind of had that idea in the back of my mind," I said. "I'll think it over some more."

"I've known a number of actors," said Aunt America. "They've all been very nice to me. And if there is anything I can do to help you, let me know."

Fortunately, I didn't say anything to the family about all this at the time. But later, when I saw that Aunt America's advice was good and calmly announced to my unsuspecting family that I was going to become an actor—all hell broke loose. But that's another story. Unfortunately, Aunt America wasn't around at the time to help me fight it out.

It was only a little over a year after she was married to Uncle Cliff that he died. Of course Mrs. Snoopy and others made comments, and said that they were certain now she would come to a bad end of some sort. It was wishful thinking on their part. When in due course of time the estate was settled and she received her share, which was a nice nest egg, she spent most of it on a trip around the world.

She came back to Marshalltown for a brief two weeks' visit and proudly displayed her loot. She had an enormous diamond ring that she said had been given her by a friend in Singapore. But he was a perfectly respectable man, as he had been born in Philadelphia. She had gifts from other friends, too, whom she had met on her travels. Eyebrows were raised, but Aunt America didn't care. She told all Cliff's relatives how much she loved them and how wonderful they had been to her—but she thought she'd go to California to live.

When she arrived in California, she wrote a letter to one of the cousins. In the letter she said she hadn't been as lonely on the long trip across the continent as she had anticipated. The first night in the diner she sat opposite "a perfectly dear old gentleman. When I told him I was a widow and shed a tear or two, he was most sympathetic. He had recently lost his wife, too, so we had much to talk about. And imagine my suprise when I learned he was Ulysses S. Grant, Jr., the eldest son of the late President. He has a wonderful hotel here in San Diego, and has arranged for me to have a lovely suite of rooms. I see him quite often, and we are the best of friends. More later. With love to all, America."

The general was sixty at the time, and Aunt America was only thirty-four. Undoubtedly he was proud to be seen in the company of such a beautiful and dashing young widow. And then the unexpected happened.

I have here on my desk at the moment an old, faded newspaper clipping. It was sent me by one of my favorite cousins, Katharyn, who was always very fond of Aunt America, too. The headlines on the long story state:

U. S. GRANT WED WEEK AGO
Secret Marriage Rends Family
Bride Is Ignored by Relatives.

The surprising announcement was made in San Diego yesterday evening that U. S. Grant, Jr., eldest son of the late soldier-President, was secretly married to Mrs. America Workman Will the night of July 12.

The story goes on to give more pertinent details. There was just as much distress among the Grant family as there had been a few years previously among Uncle Cliff's relatives. (Why everyone should have objected to Aunt America being married is something I've never understood.)

But despite the objections that the Grant family raised, and which were related in detail in the newspaper, the news story went on to say, "But Grant was firm, and the difference in their ages had nothing whatsoever to do with the love and admiration he felt for his beautiful bride." Speaking of the wedding dinner, the newspaper said of the guests present, "Mr. Grant they found very blithe and looking not within ten years of his sixty, while Mrs. Grant was happy and brilliant, and displayed her engagement ring, which is a diamond of five carats."

Shortly after they were safely married, Aunt America wrote back to Marshalltown, telling how happy she was and how everyone else should relax and be happy, too.

"Just think of our names," she wrote. "He's U. S. and I'm America —that's a combination hard to beat. And we'll live happily together ever after." [They did, too.] "I was very thrilled on the evening following the wedding announcement dinner. Some of my good husband's best friends hired a Mexican string band. They came and serenaded us outside the bridal suite at the U. S. Grant Hotel, where we will make our home. I was so pleased when they played one of my favorite songs, *There'll Be a Hot Time in the Old Town Tonight.*"

3

THE SAWDUST TRAIL

THE next unconventional person who influenced me in my school-boy days was the evangelist Billy Sunday. When I was a senior in high school, he came to Marshalltown to hold a revival. I wasn't certain at the time whether or not I was a sinner. Billy Sunday, I felt, would give me the answer.

I had already been converted when I was eleven. There had been an itinerant evangelist in town. He gave a special Sunday afternoon service especially aimed at young boys like myself. He told us all about the curse of drink, the evils of smoking, how to keep our thoughts and language clean, and other facts of life that truly amazed us. In our boyish innocence we suspected such things went on in the adult world, but we weren't quite certain, although we often discussed them among ourselves in whispers, back of the barn.

The main point of this evangelist's sermon was how a certain man indulged in all the sins of the flesh. This ultimately brought about his ruin, and in a drunken frenzy one night he murdered his boyhood sweetheart, whom he had previously ruined and hadn't even offered marriage. The evangelist told us how he went to jail and was executed for his crime, and how his aged mother sat alone at home weeping, with the lamp lighted in the window, hoping—but in vain—that some day her errant son would return to her. He had us in tears.

"Do you want your mother to suffer as this mother suffered?" pleaded the evangelist. "Do you want to bring furrows of sorrow to her sweet face, and unhappiness to her lonely heart? Come forward, ye sinners, and repent before it is too late!"

I went forward and repented. I certainly didn't want my mother waiting for me while I was in jail. She was impatient enough with me if I took an hour or more longer on an errand than she felt absolutely necessary.

But that had been a long time ago. I was just a kid then. Now I felt very grown up, but there had been a lot of things I had done in the intervening years that I'd just as soon not talk about. Maybe I needed converting all over again.

So Billy Sunday came to town to hold a real rip-snorting, old-fashioned, roof-raising revival. All the preachers in town were delighted. Billy Sunday was to them even more than the ideal evangelist. Wasn't he in a sense a home-town boy? Should he come back to Marshalltown to save the sinners, many of whom were his old boyhood friends, it would be a triumph, not only for Marshalltown, but also for Billy Sunday.

He had come to Marshalltown originally back in the 1880's, just after he had graduated from high school in a small near-by town. His first job was working for my father, who at that time was one of the partners in an undertaking parlor and furniture store. Billy Sunday drove the hearse. He also did odd jobs about the store.

In those days, according to all reports, Billy was just one of the boys. He played cards, went to the theater, used language that was strong and forceful if not always pure, and was no better and no worse than the rest of the young men about town. His sins, which he took great pleasure in confessing publicly when he became an evangelist, were the conventional ones.

He became a sensational ball player, and extremely popular with the home-town team. Now "Pop" Anson, captain of the famous Chicago White Sox, was also a Marshalltown boy, the son of one of the early settlers. On one of his visits home "Pop" saw Billy playing ball and immediately asked him to join the White Sox. Billy's friends gave him a farewell banquet, patted him on the back, and wished him luck. As stories of his great sucess drifted back to Marshalltown, they were all proud of him, and often boasted of Billy Sunday, the home-town boy who had made good. Then he was converted and became an evangelist—and what an evangelist!

He might well have been called "the acrobatic preacher." During his sermons he would turn handsprings, sometimes fall flat upon his face with all the skill of a ball player hitting third base, smash chairs, jump up and down—and then, vigorous still, yet dripping with perspiration, sink to his knees and plead with the sinners to come forward and repent.

From his first sermon I quickly learned that I was still a sinner. I danced, I played cards, and I went to the theater. I even had the leading role in the senior class play. Rehearsals were going nicely, and it looked as if the play would be a triumph for all concerned. But then came the fly in the ointment. Among Billy Sunday's co-workers, whom he brought with him, was a bright young man named Glenn Frank.

Mr. Frank was in charge of the boys' work. He heard about the play. At one of his afternoon meetings he told us in plain terms exactly how Billy Sunday felt about the theater. To Billy, the theater was a pitfall for the young, a place of evil designs and vile lusts, and even attendance at the theater led to ruin. The theater stirred our worst passions. Being stirred, we'd take to drink, and the next downward step was consorting with fallen women. There was but one thing for us to do—set an example to our friends and neighbors and our weaker brothers and sisters, and abandon the class play!

We all liked Mr. Frank. His arguments were persuasive, and he seemed a sincere, genuine person. He himself led, so he told us, a good clean life, and he intended to amount to something—but he wasn't going to be led astray by that evil institution that ruined so many young people, the theater. (Later Glenn Frank did fulfill his ambitions. He became in time Editor of the *Century Magazine*, then President of the University of Wisconsin, and was once mentioned as a candidate for President of the United States.)

What were we to do? We didn't know! We wanted to do what was right, of course. We also wanted to give our class play. And so the moments of indecision dragged on. Glenn Frank prayed with us, prayed for us, and told us what a triumph it would be if we would all come to the tabernacle in a body and be converted wholesale.

Finally our decision was made. Billy Sunday himself, in a way he didn't expect, gave us the final answer. Now, our fathers had all known him as a young man. They had played ball with him. They had been proud of his success as a member of the White Sox. And what more fitting tribute could be paid Billy Sunday than for them to give him a bang-up banquet, present him with the keys of the city, and proclaim that Billy Sunday was a regular fellow, one of them, a home-town boy who had made good.

Then on May 23 Billy Sunday preached his famous sermon "For Men Only," on booze and other things. We all went, of course, for the title of his sermon intrigued us beyond measure. That afternoon Billy Sunday gave a truly magnificent performance. He took off his coat. He jumped up and down. He tore off his shirt and threw it in the air. He shook his clenched fists at the devil. He smashed a chair. And then he knelt down and prayed.

He prayed for all his old friends, and mentioned them by name.
He spoke of my father Charlie Glick, "that old sinner who, when he
was a young man—" and so forth. He mentioned the fathers of my
friends, too, all of whom were now the leading citizens of the town.
He told us what had gone on in Marshalltown in the old days when
our fathers were young. He didn't miss a detail. He told us things
about our fathers that we had never suspected. We sat stunned—but
interested. He spotted us in the audience and made a personal plea
for us to come forward.

"Hit the sawdust trail! Don't be like your old man," he begged us.
"Come forward—all of you—and set an example to those old
sinners, your reprobate fathers!"

Now this was something to be thought over carefully. We had,
quite naturally, a loyalty to our dads. And if they really were as bad
as Billy Sunday painted them—what an opportunity he had given
us for blackmail. We didn't go forward that afternoon.

When word spread around after the service about what Billy
Sunday had said, telephones began to ring. Father, who had been
taking his usual Sunday afternoon nap, sprang into action. He told
the family that he had to go see some of his friends on an important
business matter. When he got home he asked me what I was going
to do after school the next day. I had no plans, save the usual routine.

"Good," said Father. "What say we have your Mother fix us up a
lunch basket—and just you and I go off for a picnic supper in the
country?"

"Fine," I said, wondering what he had up his sleeve.

This expedition was something quite out of the ordinary, and it
was the first time he had ever suggested anything of the sort. Father
and I were not exactly pals. We didn't share many common interests.
He liked sports and was busy all day at the office. I liked books and

music, and preferred to give shows in the backyard rather than attend the baseball games. He had never taken the time or the trouble to get acquainted, and I was something of a puzzle and a problem to him.

But that day he met me at the high school and we drove out into the country. At first, the situation was a little embarrassing for both of us. We were like a couple of strangers, who should have been friends, trying desperately hard to become acquainted.

Finally Father broke the ice by saying, "There's a woman in this town I don't like—never have."

"Why not?" I asked.

"She saw you in your cradle when you were a baby and said, 'What a large head he has. Is he smart?' "

There were two questions that popped into my mind. I asked the obvious one first, "What did you say?"

"I said, 'Damned if I know, ma'am. But he's my only son, and I'll do what I can to give him an education.' "

Then I asked the second question, "Do you think I am smart?"

"Damned if I know," Father answered. "Are you?"

"Damned if I know," I replied.

"Well, I suppose time will tell!" he said glumly.

This was good man-talk, and if he wanted to kid me a little, I was glad of it. I was pleased that he didn't take me too seriously.

Then he said, "I understand you heard Billy Sunday preach yesterday. Did you like what he said?"

"It was interesting," I replied cautiously. "He told me a lot of things I hadn't known before."

"Did you believe them?" he asked, trying to be casual.

I thought a moment before replying, and then said, "I'd like to."

Apparently he didn't quite know how I meant that remark, yet he said modestly, "Well—maybe I'm not quite as black as I've been painted."

"I don't think Billy Sunday was an angel, either, when he was a young man," I replied.

"I know damn well he wasn't!" said Father emphatically. "Has he converted you yet?"

"No, sir—not yet."

"You going to be?" Father asked.

"Should I?"

"That's something for you to decide—if you're smart, like I think you are," said Father grimly.

We drew up at the side of the road and unpacked the picnic basket Mother had prepared for us. There were fried chicken, sandwiches, fruit salad, and deviled eggs.

Father reached into his hip pocket and brought out a pint of whisky.

"On occasions like this—when the women folks aren't around—I always like a nip before eating," he said. "And the demon rum, as Billy Sunday calls it, hasn't ruined my life, either."

He wasn't defiant. He wasn't angry. He wasn't boasting. He was merely stating a fact. I admired him very much. He was somewhat like Aunt America, free and unashamed.

"Can I have a nip, too, Dad?" I asked.

He handed me the bottle, and I took a good drink.

"First time you've ever taken a drink?" he asked.

"No, sir." And I felt that the time had come to confess. It was easier confessing to Father now than it would have been to Glenn Frank, or even Billy Sunday.

"Remember that bottle of whisky that Grandfather gave you for Christmas?" I asked. "You kept it in the sideboard—and complained it was the weakest whisky you'd ever tasted? Well—I'd take a nip now and then, and fill up the bottle with water."

He looked at me in astonishment. "What a terrible thing to do to good whisky!" he said. Then he got very angry. "Look—I ought to thrash you for that! Not so much for taking a drink—but for sneaking about the bush. If you ever want a drink of my whisky— take one! If you want to smoke, too—go to the cigar store, get the biggest, strongest cigar they have. Come home. We'll get a bottle, too, and sit in the living room and drink and smoke. And if the women folks object, we won't pay any attention. If there's anything I do—you're entitled to do it, too. Get that straight?"

"Yes, sir," I said meekly, and I was very pleased with him.

Somehow he made my problem much easier. As I nibbled on the fried chicken I came to my decision.

"Billy Sunday claims the theater is sinful," I said. "And Glenn Frank wants us to give up our class play."

"So I've heard," said Father soberly.

"Well," I said, "I guess we're going to do it."

"Do what?"

"Give the class play—and not be converted!"

Father smiled happily. He put his arm around my shoulder affectionately and said, "You're a son after my own heart—and I'm proud of you. I'm glad you came to this decision all by yourself. Here, help yourself," and he handed me the bottle.

Then he went on to say, "Now you've told me this—I'll tell you something. After that sermon yesterday, some of us got together and talked things over. We had planned a big banquet for Billy Sunday —but we're calling it off. Not that we're sore about what he said yesterday. Everybody knows all those things about us, anyway."

I grinned and made no reply.

"We all work hard, and pay our debts, try to make an honest living, and do all we can to keep this a decent town in which to bring up our children—and we don't take a holier-than-thou attitude, either! And none of us is as sorry over what we did years ago as Billy Sunday is. We just feel he's much too good a man now to associate with us old sinners, and we wouldn't like to embarrass him!"

Then he said emphatically, "And another thing, we decided yesterday that if all of you gave up the class play and got converted, we'd thrash you! We can do it, too! Now it's up to all of you to make your class play the best ever given at the Opera House—and we'll all be there to applaud you!"

4

"10-20-30"

ON THE night that the highly moral, romantic old melodrama *The Lady of Lyons* was given at the Opera House, the theater was packed to the rafters. All our fathers and mothers, aunts and uncles and friends were present, clad in their best bib and tucker. They laughed at exactly the right places, applauded until they almost got blisters on their hands, and cheered us vigorously when the final curtain fell. To many in the audience it didn't matter in the least that, only a few blocks down the street that same evening, Billy Sunday was delivering a sermon on the evils of the theater.

But perhaps Billy Sunday was right. For when I read the review of the play in the newspaper the next day, I was certainly ruined. You see, the paper said that in the leading role in the play I displayed marked ability, and that my "portrayal would compare very favorably with that of some professional actors who have been seen here in the part"!

The trouble was that I believed it! I immediately had my picture taken in the costumes I wore that night, and started keeping a scrapbook. Then I announced to the family that my mind was made up. Fame and fortune awaited me. I was going to become an actor!

Then the storm broke. Mother was practically in tears. There had never been an actor in her Quaker family. Aunt Rachel deplored the fact that I had not been converted by Billy Sunday. Father said that that had nothing to do with the matter, but he wanted to have a talk with me. And Grandmother thought that I'd better have an extra dose of Peruna.

Father and I took another ride into the country.

"I want you to do what you want, of course," he said. "And whatever you do, promise me to do it to the best of your ability. Even though you turn out to be a bank robber—and I hope you won't—be a good one! But I'd like you to go into business with me."

Having sold out his interest in the furniture store, Father was now a manufacturer of gasoline engines and furnaces.

"I don't want to spend my life among machines," I said. "I hate them!"

"Sometimes I don't get too much pleasure out of them, either," he replied truthfully. "But I've got to do something for a living, and so I carry on. This is a fine town, Carl. All your friends are here, and it's your home. What sort of a life would you have if you were an actor—a different town every night—and hotels to live in?"

"But I'd be doing what I want to do," I argued. "If I'm to be a writer, as Mother wants me to be, and write plays, how can I know about the theater unless I'm an actor first? That's what Aunt America advised."

Father practically jumped out of his skin at that. "Good Lord," he exclaimed, "don't bring her name into this argument. If the women folks knew she advised you like that, there'd be all hell to pay—and it's difficult enough as it is."

"I'll never mention her again," I said. "But I still think she's right."

"And I don't see much sense in your wanting to be a writer, either," said Father glumly. "Although your teacher has told me she thinks you may have some talent along those lines. But writers always starve to death."

And so we Glicks had many a stormy family session. Finally we came to a compromise of a sort—but that was only because I had a letter in my pocket that showed me how I could, in a sense, have my cake and eat it, too.

Father said, "Before you make up your mind what to do, I wish you'd go to college first. I have always been sorry I was never able to graduate from college—and that has been a great disappointment to your grandfather."

Father's college career had come to a most abrupt end. He had been expelled. He preferred playing baseball to studying, and he took part in pranks which simply weren't done in the small church school he attended.

Now Father selected for me Northwestern University, a good Methodist school. It couldn't have been a happier choice, because in near-by Chicago there was an actor, Donald Robertson, from whom I had had the letter that the family didn't know about.

Donald Robertson led a company of players who held forth at the Chicago Art Institute. He toured the surrounding country, too, and often played in Marshalltown. Since he appeared in nothing but the classics, it was always considered an intellectual and uplifting evening when he came to town. He was dignified. He was Art.

I had written him a letter telling him that I was going to Northwestern in the fall and asking him if there was a chance of his taking me into his company in my spare time. In reply I received a letter from his secretary, who later I learned was also his wife, wanting to know if I had had any previous stage experience, my age, height, weight, and expected salary.

I answered immediately, saying that, while I had had no professional experience, still I had played the leading roles in all the high school plays for the last four years, was even at the moment engaged in writing a play which I hoped would be suitable for him, and added, "I am five (5) feet eleven (11) inches high, nineteen (19) years of age, and weigh one hundred and thirty-six pounds, and salary is no consideration."

Robertson replied, saying that when I was in Chicago I should come and see him at the Art Institute, which I hastened to do at the very first opportunity.

On the stage Donald Robertson often played comedy roles, and his bluff, hearty manner made him seem a friendly, jovial, and kindly person. But off the stage I found him terrifying. He had a habit of blinking his eyes, staring directly at you, and mumbling "Hm" with an air of finality that I left you speechless.

When I was first ushered into his presence and told him I had written him, he gave me a cold, calm appraisal and said, "Hm—so you are he! Have you ever read blank verse?"

"Yes, sir," I managed to stammer. "For practice I've read aloud *The Iliad, The Odyssey, Paradise Lost,* and all the plays of Shakespeare, including the sonnets."

He blinked several times, mumbled "Hm," and handed me a copy of Molière's *Tartuffe,* saying, "Read some of this."

I did, quaking in my boots. It was a terrible experience. My whole future life depended upon my making a favorable impression. If I should fail—it would be the end for me. For a moment I almost wished I had been converted by Billy Sunday. But I took a deep breath, said a prayer, and started to read. I thought he was going to let me go on forever. But finally he stopped me.

"You have an Iowa accent," he said, "but we can change that. I've a bit part in the last act—the Officer. How much salary do you want?"

It was my turn to stare at him and blink. But finally I managed to stammer, "I hadn't thought."

He waited politely while I came back to earth and had collected my senses.

"It costs me ten cents carfare from Evanston each way," I said. "Then I'll have to have dinner in Chicago on the nights we play— that's fifty cents. Would seventy-five cents a performance be too much?"

"Hm—hm," he said. "Hm! We'll compromise for two dollars, as you'll have to buy your own make-up. I'll furnish the costumes. Tell me—do you wet your pants?"

"No, sir—not any more," I replied truthfully.

"Last season I had a college boy playing bit parts—and every time he got nervous he'd wet his pants. If you do that, you'll have to pay for cleaning your costume—out of your salary."

"Yes, sir," I said.

"Rehearsal at one o'clock—be on time!"

"Thank you, sir!" I said.

When I got out of the Art Institute the sun was shining—the skies were blue—and what a beautiful, beautiful world it was. I was now an actor—a professional actor! I was being paid for it! I was walking on clouds—but my knees gave way, and I sat down on the steps of the Art Institute. I had twenty-eight lines of blank verse. And right then and there I read them aloud. Some people passing by gave me peculiar stares, but I didn't mind in the least.

However, at the rehearsal none of the company paid the least bit of attention to me. They seemed totally unaware of the historical significance of the occasion—the first appearance on the professional stage of one of the future great stars of the American theater, who would also write his own plays. But I suppose it was the same when Shakespeare, Molière, and other geniuses made their debuts.

However, at the second rehearsal the leading lady, beautiful Margaret Moreland, did condescend to speak to me. I had just finished saying my lines.

"Tell me," she said. "Are you getting paid for this?"

"Yes, ma'am," I replied proudly. "Two dollars!"

"It's too much!" she said.

Nothing momentous happened on the night of the opening performance. I said my lines, and received my two dollars. The next play was Calderon's *The Mayor of Zalamaya*, and I was cast in the role of King Philip II of Spain. I had a gorgeous costume—authentic, too. There was a long mirror in the hall outside the dressing room, and I'd stand there admiring myself and striking appropriate poses. One evening in the midst of my solitary enjoyment of my Narcissus complex I was brought sharply back to earth.

Behind me I heard the deep, booming voice of Donald Robertson saying, "The King of Spain may have had thin legs—but bigawd, he kept his stockings pulled up."

On the program I was listed as Herman Glick. I didn't want the family to know, and felt that "Herman" was disguise enough—but human vanity being what it is, I used my real last name. One evening when I made my appearance upon the stage, I heard a surprised squeal from the audience. I thought my stockings were down again, but somehow I managed to say my lines. When the play was over, I was told that there were two ladies waiting to see me. One was a cousin from Marshalltown, and the other was Carrie Jacobs Bond, who wrote, among other popular songs, *The End of a Perfect Day.*

"I certainly was surprised when I saw you," squealed my cousin. "But why do you call yourself Herman?"

"Because I don't want the family to know," I replied, and I asked her not to tell.

"I most certainly will," she said. "You did beautifully. I heard every word you said!"

"To be a member of Donald Robertson's company is for you an artistic triumph!" exclaimed Mrs. Bond forcefully. "But use your own name. I do—all of it! And acting is just as honorable a profession as composing songs!"

Which was, of course, a word of cheer. But the cat was now out of the bag, and I could no longer go about in my disguise as an actor. Somehow or other I had to calm down the family.

I wrote home to Father, saying that I was being paid two dollars a performance. Then I asked him not to send me any more money, as I would try and support myself on my salary. I mailed the letter in fear and trembling, lest he take me at my word. But I felt that the gesture was a noble one on my part, and I was confident that the thought would appeal to Father. He wrote back, wanting to know just how much I had made to date. I told him the truth, and added that I had profits totaling $1.25 on each appearance. That won him over. He sent me a check equaling my salary to date.

My Aunt Alice was living in Chicago at that time. She had social ambitions. So I sent her tickets and a program, checking with a red pencil the imposing list of patrons of Donald Robertson's Company of Players. These included the very flower of Chicago's Four Hundred, some of the most prominent persons in the city. Aunt Alice came to see me in a play and applauded vigorously. To Mrs. Bond's comment that my triumph was artistic, she added that it was also a triumph socially.

Now Mother had a certain weakness, too. She was an awful sucker when it came to fortunetellers. She went to them regularly, and believed every word they told her. She even believed Aunt Rachel, who read fortunes in tea leaves.

So I inquired of friends and was told of a Chicago fortuneteller who everybody said was amazing. It was my first experience with that sort of hocus-pocus. Fortunetelling, I felt, was all right for women, who never could make up their minds anyway. But it was absurd for a man. Being captain of my fate and master of my soul, what could a fortuneteller tell me about myself that I didn't already know?

When I rapped on the door, a huge amazon of a woman greeted me. I decided not to make a single scoffing comment, as it was obvious that she could easily throw me out on my ear. She led me into the living room. I don't know what I expected—perhaps oriental trappings of some sort, dim lights, and incense sticks in huge bowls. But it was a plain, ordinary sitting room. Crayon portraits of her family were hanging on the walls, a funeral wreath in a glass frame over the mantel, and there were chairs and a table on which reposed a Bible. I was disappointed. But we sat down at the table, facing each other. Then she went into a trance, groaned and moaned a bit, and called upon her guiding spirit—which, she said, was an Indian chief.

"Come, come, gentle spirit, talk to me," she mumbled. "This young man is troubled. He has sore problems. He needs aid, advice, and comfort. Yes, yes, guiding spirit, I am listening. You say you see this young man moving about making many gestures. He is very active. Maybe you see him a clerk in a store, tying up packages. Am I right, young man?"

"No ma'am," I said. "I'm an actor. That explains the gestures."

"Yes, yes, spirit guide, you are right. I see it now. He is an actor.

But he does not know whether he should continue to be an actor. Is that right?"

"Quite right," I answered. "Mother wants me to be a writer—but I think I should be an actor first."

"Spirit guide, talk to me," moaned the fortuneteller. "Tell me about this young man. At present he is an actor, but I see him someday being a writer. His mother is unhappy. Should he be a writer, spirit? Yes, yes, guiding spirit, he should be a writer and will have success if he works hard." She came out of her trance, opened her eyes, smiled at me, and said, "One dollar, please!"

It was well worth it. She had told me exactly what I wanted to know. I thanked her and went my way. When I wrote Mother about this visit to the fortuneteller, she was very pleased. She replied that the medium had told me the truth, and that when she came to Chicago the medium was the first person she wanted to meet. She also added that Aunt Rachel had read the tea leaves, and they said that it was all right for me to be an actor at the moment, but not to take it too seriously, and study hard, and someday I'd be a writer.

So I continued my acting career, and on the next program I used my own name. It was Carl Glick who played the role of the Earl of Leicester in Sheridan's *The Critic*. And, since Donald Robertson always cast me as kings, earls, and nobles of one sort or another, the family were quite happy. Such dignified parts! It was even educational.

Then one day the most amazing thing happened. I was at rehearsal that Saturday morning as usual. After the company had been dismissed for lunch, Donald Robertson called me to one side.

"This is in perfect confidence," he said.

"Yes, sir," I replied.

"I presume you wish to continue your career as an actor?"

The thought flashed through my head that he was going to fire me, so I said hastily, "Yes, sir—and I'll know my lines after lunch."

But he continued, saying, "Next year I am going to send out a company playing *Romeo and Juliet*—and I offer you the role of Romeo. It is the opportunity of a lifetime."

I was speechless. Words failed me, and I could only stare at him in open-mouthed wonder.

"There is no need at the moment for you to say anything," he went on. "Think it over. Instead of two dollars a performance, the salary will be twenty-five dollars a week."

He stalked away, leaving me standing beside the statue of a wolf clinging to a lion's back. In less time than it takes me to write this line, I thought it over. The answer was yes. To hell with college! I was flunking Latin and a couple of other courses anyway. Now I could travel, see the world, meet people, and it would all be grist to the mill for the day when I became a playwright.

Of course the family raised a questioning eyebrow. But since twenty-five dollars a week was more than some of the workers in the factory received, Father was rather impressed.

Mother said that she hoped I wouldn't become conceited, like most actors. But she added that acting in one of Shakespeare's plays was certainly better than being in some of the awful cheap melodramas that came to the Opera House occasionally.

"My club spent one entire winter reading and studying Shakespeare. His plays all point a fine moral, and contain some wonderful philosophy. But certainly if the play wasn't an immortal classic like *Romeo and Juliet*, I'd put my foot down strong!"

Aunt Rachel, however, was tearful about the whole thing. She didn't believe me when I told her that the company would be composed of Christian ladies and gentlemen who would attend church every Sunday.

"I've been going to church every Sunday for years," she said, "and I've never yet seen an actor in church. You'll probably learn to drink, smoke, swear, and do other terrible things, too. You were such a nice, clean-minded little boy—and now look at you—an actor!"

My sister Charlotte's only comment was, "Romeo! With those skinny legs of yours, you'll look funny in tights!"

The next September, off I went to Chicago. It was a tearful farewell at the railroad station.

After two weeks of rehearsal, we gave our first performance in a small town in Wisconsin. Then we started on a tour of the Middle West. We were what was known in those days as a "tank town troupe," which meant we played one-night stands. We had no regular bookings and didn't know from one week to the next just where we'd be. It was called "wildcatting."

The manager of the company was Colonel James B. Davis. I never knew whether he really had once been a colonel or whether the title was an honorary one of his own selection. But certainly he looked the part; a ponderous, dignified, penny-pinching gentleman with iron-gray hair. The first thing upon arriving in every town, he'd play solitaire to determine whether or not there'd be enough money in the box office that night to pay the railroad fare of the company to the next town. And after the evening performance he'd again play solitaire to console himself with the hope of better receipts at the next stop.

He had as his advance agent, publicity director, and business manager, Homer Drake. Homer would travel ahead of the company and, on arriving in a town, would try to sell the manager of the local opera house the appearance at his theater of our company for a percentage of gross receipts. Once he had signed the contract, Homer would hire some small boys and go from billboard to billboard putting up posters announcing:

Extraordinary Engagement for
ONE NIGHT ONLY
of
THE ASSOCIATE PLAYERS COMPANY
in
Shakespeare's Immortal Tragedy of Love and Passion
Romeo and Juliet
with
Margaret Bucklin as Juliet and Carl Glick as Romeo
A Great Scenic Production Elaborately Staged

Aunt Rachel was very much afraid that I would fall in love with Juliet and marry her. But I hastened to assure her that she need have no fears. Margaret Bucklin once played with Modjeska, and with that as a clue it is easy to guess her age. I felt that she was old enough to be my mother. And she behaved like one—bossed me around, told me to wear my rubbers, and at the slightest sign of a sniffle, made me take a dose of castor oil.

Colonel Davis hinted once that it would be wise for us not to be seen together on the street, for townspeople might think we really were mother and son. But at the theater, when she put on her blonde wig and slapped on her make-up, Margaret Bucklin didn't look too much older than I did. She coached me in my lines, gave me sound, solid advice on acting, and was a sincere, honest, and loyal friend.

The actress playing the role of the nurse was something of a problem. There was no mistaking her age. She had once been in burlesque, but now past the age of the strip-tease she played character parts as if her life depended upon it.

She was really one of the best Nurses I've ever seen in *Romeo and Juliet*—for she did all the true-and-tried tricks of burlesque, slapped her thighs, lifted up her skirts, and made the character completely rowdy.

"Give 'em a laugh," she'd say. "There's enough gloom in this old chestnut of a play. It may be art with a capital A—but then, so is burlesque—and that's where I learned the business."

Miss Bucklin thought her very vulgar, and soon they weren't speaking. I didn't get along with Friar Laurence, either. He was a seasoned old trouper with a lean, melancholy face, long hair (which he wore in the style of Sir Henry Irving), and a strut that proclaimed him an actor without any further questions asked. He had a coat with a fur collar and always carried a walking stick. And how he loved to parade up and down the main street, giving the natives a chance to admire him off the stage. What he thought of my acting is unmentionable. He knew every part in every play that Shakespeare had ever written, and claimed he could play any one of the roles on ten minutes' notice. But he was too old for Romeo. He'd constantly write me notes, telling me what a thoroughly bad actor I was and how much better other Romeos with whom he had played had been. I put it down to professional jealousy and let it go at that.

It was a wonderful experience—a different town every day. But all I can remember about the towns we played in is, now and then, a hotel or a theater, which might be either awful or very good. I remember some fine dressing rooms. But one town I shall never forget is Marshfield, Wisconsin. It was on a Saturday night, and the theater was packed—fortunately, for that meant we'd be paid and also have carfare to the next town.

The play was going very well, and then came the balcony scene. As usual, we felt the audience was most attentive, and the boys and girls were all holding hands and sighing blissfully as they listened to the impassioned utterances of the immortal lovers.

The Nurse called Juliet. "Sweet Montague, be true," whispered Juliet in a loud voice. "Stay but a little, I will come again."

I was alone on the stage. The business at that moment required me to turn toward the footlights, hold forth my arms in a rapturous gesture, and say, "O blessed, blessed night!"

No sooner had I spoken the words, than a loud, raucous voice yelled from the balcony, "I'll tell the world it is!"

"O blessed, blessed night," echoed the entire balcony, and immediately went into a cheer, "Good old Marshfield, fight and win. Rah! Rah! Rah!!!"

The rest of the audience cheered, too. It seemed that Marshfield had won the football game that day. From that moment on, every time I tried to say a line, the raucous voice would yell, "Tell us again, Romeo, what a blessed, blessed night this is!"

Finally the curtain fell on the scene. Miss Bucklin was about ready to have hysterics—but what could we do? The next scene was the long soliloquy of Friar Laurence, and did he have a chance to say a single line? He did not.

"We want Romeo!" cried the balcony. "Tell us again what a blessed, blessed night this is. We want Romeo! Rah! Rah! Rah!"

We had to ring down the curtain. Colonel Davis stepped before the footlights and made a speech. The manager of the opera house, together with a policeman, hurried to the balcony. Order was restored. But the entire company was on edge. We didn't know when they might want Romeo again.

Then came the final tomb scene. I said my lines, drank the poison, flopped on my back on the stage, and was grateful that, so far as I was concerned, this evening was at last over. Juliet in her final lines was unduly emotional.

"Oh, happy dagger," she murmured, and meant it. "This is thy sheath; there rust, and let me die." She stabbed herself in a thoroughly realistic manner, and then collapsed on my supposedly dead body. Now we had rehearsed this business so that she always fell across my chest. But this night she fell right on top of my stomach, and heavily. The inevitable happened. Up in the air went my legs, I waved my arms in desperation, and said, "Oh, migawd!"

Roar after roar of laughter surged through the audience. "We want Romeo!" chanted the balcony. "O blessed, blessed night," yelled others. The curtain fell. As far as I know, the audience is still laughing.

But on we jogged, and week after week Colonel Davis was owing each and every one of us more and more on last week's unpaid salary. In one town in North Dakota the critic on the local paper said in his review, "After seeing Margaret Bucklin as Juliet and Carl Glick as Romeo in the immortal love tragedy last night we are convinced it was Bacon and not Shakespeare who wrote the play"!

Eight weeks later we managed to limp into Madison, Wisconsin. Some twenty persons came to the matinee. Three bought tickets for the evening performance, so Colonel Davis decided it wasn't even worth while ringing up the curtain. We were stranded.

The company hadn't been paid recently, and none of us had

too much money. But we pooled our resources and managed to get carfare back to Chicago. I was broke, and had to pawn practically the shirt off my back. I didn't even have an I.O.U. from Colonel Davis for the unpaid salary he owed me. He hold me to phone him at his office, which I did, twice a day. But he was always out, and I never saw him again.

I managed to borrow some money from my college fraternity brothers in Evanston. Also Aunt Alice was good enough to give me a free meal now and then. Father sent me a check, and urged me to come home. But I was still stubborn. I did the usual running around to theatrical agencies, but with no success.

Then one evening an old friend from Marshalltown, Jessie Binford, who was associated with Jane Addams at Hull House invited me to dinner. Her work at Hull House was dealing with what today we call "juvenile delinquents." We had a long talk. She said that if I wanted to be an actor, that was my privilege. But if I stubbed my toes and fell flat upon my face, the thing to do was to pick myself up as best I could, look at myself in the mirror, and then make my own decision what to do next. And as long as I didn't get arrested, the only thing she could do for me was to give advice.

But she did suggest that two blocks away from Hull House was the Bijou Theater, where a stock company popularly priced at "10–20–30" cents—10 cents in the gallery, 20 cents in the balcony, and all of 30 cents in the orchestra—was playing melodramas, the *On the Bridge at Midnight* type of play. Jessie Binford said that, while it might not be as dignified as playing in Shakespeare, still the company was a good one, and why didn't I go and see the manager? I did, and luck was with me.

The play for the next week was that lurid thriller *No Mother to Guide Her*. I was offered the small part of Parson Thomas—at a salary of ten dollars a week. And the manager promised me that if I made good I could also play in the next bill, that famous and shocking play *Sappho*.

It would never do for the family to know about this. Understanding and sympathetic, Jessie Binford promised not to tell.

I lived across the street from the theater, in a run-down, third-rate hotel. It was inhabited by girls from the burlesque theater a few blocks down the street, their permanent and transient boy friends, and other shady and dubious characters. I paid seven dollars a week for my room, which left me three dollars for food and laundry. But I soon learned that in the bar, for two glasses of beer at five cents each, I could have all the free lunch I wanted: kippered herring, cheese sandwiches, and dill pickles.

During the week of rehearsal I made the acquaintance of one of these burlesque queens. Her name was Sylvia. Weighing over two hundred pounds, she was what was known as a "beef truster." Sylvia, forty if she was a day, had dyed red hair, but her heart was of pure gold. She thought it was ridiculous that I was playing the role of Father Thomas at the Bijou for only ten dollars a week. Why didn't I go into burlesque? There was more money in it—and she suggested that we work up an act together.

Although I was pledged first to appear at the Bijou, I discussed the matter freely with Sylvia. What my future might have been following the opening night at the Bijou, I do not know. Fate, destiny, misfortune—call it what you will—appeared one night at the theater in the person of a Chicago drama critic whose initials were "H.D." He came down to see the play, and wrote it up in detail in the Chicago *Inter-Ocean*.

He said in part, "After witnessing *No Mother to Guide Her* one can see at once it does not pay in the end to be a safe-blower, a murderer, a house-breaker, and a trifler with woman's love. John Livingston tried to get away with it, but at 10:20 he got fooled. He was arrested in a hut in the hills by a New York policeman in full uniform and was yanked away, hurling curses through his teeth and perspiring freely. At the same time the curly-haired and virtuous young gent who had been sent to Sing Sing, the Tombs, the City Hospital, and several other educational institutions as a result of John Livingston's intrigue stood in the center of the stage with the blonde lady, whom both men loved madly, held tightly in his arms.

"If the play were correctly named it would have been entitled *No Mother to Guide Her or Any of the Rest of Them*, because everybody in the cast would have been better off if they had had some parental advice at the right moment. . . . Even Parson Thomas, would never have performed that midnight wedding ceremony in the pale moonlight, if his mother had been notified of it in time!"

This was the most truthful review I've ever had. And the most damaging. Why Aunt Alice had to read that particular story is something I shall never understand. But she did. Immediately she came to see me. Ladies in those days did not venture freely into the wilds of Chicago around Halstead Street, save on errands of mercy to Hull House. But Aunt Alice was not the timid type. She inquired for me at the theater, learned where I was living, and appeared at the hotel. She found me in the bar, having a free lunch and talking to my good friend Sylvia about our proposed burlesque act.

Aunt Alice almost fainted when I introduced her to Sylvia.

Sylvia, in her most charming and breezy manner, said, "Glad to meet you, dearie. Sit down and have a beer."

Aunt Alice looked at Sylvia. She looked at me. But, being well housebroken socially, she sat down. She politely declined the beer, however. Aunt Alice was normally garrulous, but this day she was strangely silent. She waited for one of us to open the conversation. Sylvia rose to the occasion.

"Ain't it hell, what the paper said?" murmured Sylvia. "That damned reporter. It's terrible."

"Terrible," echoed Aunt Alice. Then went into the great silence again.

"I tell Carl," Sylvia continued, "he ought to give up the Bijou and go into burlesque with me. I've got an idea for a real snappy act. Look at me—I weigh two hundred. He's skinny. We'll do a husband and wife routine. I'll wear a snappy kimono with just enough leg showing to make it look good. We'll fix him up in a red wig, a big nose, and whiskers. Then a Lord Fauntleroy suit, velvet knee pants, a shirt with flowing tie—and won't he look funny?"

"Very funny," gasped Aunt Alice.

I felt beads of perspiration gathering on my forehead, but there was no stopping Sylvia now.

"We'll get some cute lines. Nothing raw, you understand, but real cute, with a dirty meaning if you've got a dirty mind. He'll be a henpecked husband. I'll boss him around, slap him down, and kick him in the rear now and then. But the punch will come when he'll get good and sore, grab a prop lamp, and begin to beat me on the fanny. Can't you just see it?"

Aunt Alice closed her eyes and shuddered. I mopped my brow with my handkerchief and tried to appear relaxed.

"I'll yell and scream," continued Sylvia. "Then I'll do a prat fall on the stage, do a couple of quick turns over on my face, and he'll keep paddling me until the curtain falls. Won't that be a scream of an act? Married men love that sort of roughhouse—and if you don't believe me, just ask your husband. I think we'll go over big as a team. How does the idea strike you, dearie?"

Now Aunt Alice had been at one time President of the Iowa State Federation of Women's Clubs. She was a gifted speaker, and could talk fluently and at great length upon practically any subject. But this day words failed her completely. She looked at Sylvia in stony silence. She looked at me. She rose with great dignity.

"I must be going home," she said, briefly and to the point.

"Glad to have met you, dearie," said Sylvia graciously. "It sure is a great treat meeting and talking to an educated lady like yourself. And if you have any ideas on how to improve the act—let Carl and me know. We welcome your suggestions."

"Thank you, dear," said Aunt Alice sportingly. "Thank you!"

When she arrived home safely, she immediately wired Father. And then came a deluge of telegrams and letters from the family.

They were disgraced. They were humiliated. I had cast a blot of shame upon the family honor. Playing with Donald Robertson and being Romeo in Shakespeare's play was something they could mention to their friends. But acting in burlesque with some impossible creature! Had I lost my mind? What was I going to do next? Was I going to team up with Sylvia, or was I going to appear in that immoral and terrible play *Sappho?*

Poor dear Aunt Rachel was on the verge of a nervous breakdown. Every night she put a lamp in the window to guide me safely home. She didn't sleep nights. She wept all the time. She urged me to read in the Bible the story of the Prodigal Son.

It was Thanksgiving week, but on that day I dined alone at the bar on kippered herring, cheese sandwiches, and dill pickles. I thought of the fatted calf awaiting me at home. I was hungry and lonely. I was in debt to Father and to others. I was a homesick, tired, and bewildered boy. I was a trifle disillusioned, too, about the theater.

I had thought I'd meet people in traveling about the country. But we got into a town so hurriedly and left so quickly that I hadn't gotten to know a soul outside the company. And half of them weren't speaking to the other half. And I really didn't want to wear a Lord Fauntleroy suit and have Sylvia kick me in the pants now and then while the audience roared its approval. I didn't quite see how I could learn to write plays that way.

I had had my fling. It hadn't turned out as I had expected. Perhaps Father was right. Perhaps I had better go back to college and get an education of sorts. Perhaps there were other ways of learning how to write plays than being an actor.

I sent a telegram, saying that I was coming home, and asked that the fatted calf be waiting—but since I hadn't had a real Thanksgiving Dinner, please, instead of beef, make it turkey!

5

AN APPLE A DAY

RETURNING home, however, did not mean going back to Marshall-town. In the meantime, while I had been away, Father had decided to retire from business. He sold his interest in the factory and bought an apple ranch in the Bitter Root Valley in Montana. He had been tempted by beautiful folders gotten out by a scheming land company, showing how, if you bought a ranch at one thousand dollars an acre, all you did was to go trout fishing in the mountain creeks while the big, red apples grew and ripened all by their little selves on nice, green trees. By the carload tired Easterners flocked west to relax in comfort and live the happy, carefree lives of gentlemen ranchers.

The folders didn't lie when they said that the Bitter Root Valley was a heavenly spot in which to live. Our ranch was high on a hill, overlooking the sleepy town of Hamilton. For miles to the north and south we could see the green sweep of the orchards in the valley, and surrounding us on all sides were the snow-capped mountains. The winters were mild. The summers were cool. What an ideal place in which to forget the cares of the world and let nature take its course!

But it didn't work out that way. The first summer the gross returns in fine, luscious, fragrant apples was forty dollars an acre.

For an investment of one thousand dollars, to make only forty! It didn't make sense to Father, who was, after all, primarily a business-man. He advertised the ranch for sale. But the boom had died down, and now there were no buyers. There was but one thing to do—make the best of a bad bargain and hope for better luck next year.

It was the same with all the other Easterners. But were they downhearted? No. Even though the savings of years were slowly melting away, everybody kept his chin up. They all led the sort of lives they had been accustomed to back home. Every Saturday night there was a dance at the hotel. There were dinner parties, luncheons, and picnics up the canyon. Let the apples grow as best they could; the gentlemen ranchers, to the amusement of the natives, put on evening clothes, went to the dances and parties, and had a wonderful time. It was fiddling while Rome burned.

Here I felt was an idea for a play. There were strange, startling contrasts between the natives and the "foreigners," as they called us. Up the road a bit from our ranch was the perfect orchard. The old-timers who lived here had a tumbled-down house, unpainted, with a bare and unadorned lawn, dirty and unkempt. We had a green lawn surrounding our house, and a lawn mower, which some of the natives thought was the damnedest thing to have around a ranch. We even had rose bushes and a flower garden, which Aunt Rachel tended with loving care.

Our neighbor's orchard was, unlike their home, a model of neat-ness and cleanliness. The rows between the trees were so carefully furrowed that the soil was like sand on a bathing beach. Their trees were carefully pruned and trimmed, and looked like gracious ladies attending a tea party.

Our orchard was not as neat as our lawn. Weeds grew in abundance, and we never seemed able to get rid of them. Our trees were lopsided, and we always seemed to prune the wrong branches.

The natives themselves and the lives they led were just as different from the Easterners as were their orchards and houses. While we were sociable and friendly, the natives were true to form—aloof and reserved. But I felt, since I might write a play, that my first step should be to get to know them. So, while the weeds grew in the orchard and the apples ripened in their own sweet way, armed with a notebook I went around asking questions. This made some of the natives mad, and they did everything but sick their dogs on me. Others, however, were perfectly willing to talk, and since I always started a conversation by asking how to raise apples, I usually got an answer. I really collected a lot of information about ranching, which I passed along to Father for what it was worth. And from asking questions about apple raising, I'd try to lead around to something personal. That was where the natives shut up like clams. Apparently my technique must have been wrong.

As one rancher said to Father one day, meeting him in town, "That son of yours is the damnedest, most curious, pryingest individual I ever met. I don't mind answering his questions about ranching, but when he asks me questions about my wife and kids, I don't like it. If he does it again, I'll punch him in the nose!"

However, I had much better luck with my sister's beaux. She was very beautiful—and knew it. And she had had beaux of one sort or another ever since she had been old enough to know what it was all about—which was fairly young. Charlotte was now blossoming into full-blown womanhood, very blonde, with pink cheeks. Naturally she was surrounded by lovesick young men. On the flimsiest excuse they'd drop by during the day, just so that they could have

the chance to look at her and moon a bit. Father always took them
into the orchard and put them to work. Naturally, with a mar-
riageable daughter, the entire family took a keen interest in her
conquests.

There was one young, handsome, bronzed rancher whom she met
at a dance at the hotel and found more than usually interesting.

"Invite him to dinner some evening," suggested Mother.

"I will not!" said Charlotte. "And have all of you sit and look
him over? He'd be embarrassed—for while he's awfully nice, he's
very shy, too. I'll have him come and spend an evening with me
alone—and the rest of you can just keep out of the way."

The day of his visit Charlotte spent in the kitchen. She made
a huge platter of fudge, a bowl of popcorn dipped in molasses, a
plate of sandwiches, a cake, and lemonade to wash it all down.
A feast of no mean proportions awaited Randolph. The living room
was cleaned and dusted. And the family promised to stay out of the
way.

Randolph, dressed in his best suit, arrived promptly at eight.
The family, after being properly introduced, made excuses and
vanished. We sat in the kitchen and wondered how the young
people were getting along.

At a quarter to nine we heard the front door close with a bang.
Charlotte came into the kitchen. She was in tears.

"Whatever happened?" asked Mother anxiously.

"I'm never going to invite him here again," sobbed Charlotte.

"Why not?" snapped Father.

"I asked him to have some fudge," said Charlotte, wiping the
tears from her eyes. "I offered him the sandwiches I spent all day
preparing. I asked him to have some cake. But he said—he said—"

"What?" asked Mother.

"He said, 'No thank you. I've cleaned my teeth for the night.' "

While collectively these swains of Charlotte's got in our hair, individually I found them interesting. Naturally, if I wrote a play about the Bitter Root, I'd have to have a love interest. So from the sidelines I made my own observations upon Charlotte's sweethearts and wrote character sketches about them and their behavior. These I filed away, with the notation, "Notes to be used later and enlarged upon." I spent many a solitary hour in my room writing.

"What are you doing in there all by yourself, all day long?" asked Charlotte.

"Writing."

"Writing what—letters to Sylvia?"

Aunt Alice had written to Mother about Sylvia, of course, and Mother had been worried. And she was never quite convinced when I told her that Sylvia had been only an interesting and unique character, about whom I thought I might write a story someday.

But now I had to give Charlotte some sort of a truthful answer, so I replied, "No. I'm writing a play."

"About what?"

"About life in the Bitter Root." And, hoping once and for all to silence her, I added, "I'm putting you into it, too—and all your varied and assorted sweethearts."

"Good gracious!" she gasped, and seemed genuinely frightened.

I also wrote character sketches of the family, and mentioned, sometimes kindly, sometimes blisteringly, what I felt were their eccentricities and peculiarities. I even wrote in detail the story of the time Aunt Rachel got drunk.

This happened, however, quite accidentally. As was becoming with gentlemen ranchers, on cold afternoons Father and I always liked a refreshing cup of tea. And without Aunt Rachel or Mother knowing it, we'd manage to sweeten it with a shot of brandy.

One afternoon as Aunt Rachel sipped her tea, she said to Father, "Is this a new brand? It has the most unusual and pleasant flavor."

Father and I looked at each other. We knew what had happened. Somehow, Aunt Rachel had gotten the wrong cup.

"Yes," said Father, not batting an eye. "It's something quite new. Like it?"

"Delicious! Delicious!" murmured Aunt Rachel.

"Let me fix you another cup," I said.

"Do, please."

So I did, and put in an extra-large shot of brandy.

"It's wonderful," said Aunt Rachel.

The third cup had even more brandy.

Aunt Rachel began to giggle. "I feel sort of lightheaded," she stuttered. "It's the altitude. But it's never affected me like thish before. I think I'll lie down—I feel funnies—"

We held our breath as she staggered up the stairs.

Immediately Mother was suspicious. "Let me smell that cup!" she exclaimed. She was very angry. "You should not have done this— I'm going to see if she is all right."

Father and I were both shamefaced when Mother came back.

It was stories like that which I wrote and put away among my notes. But Charlotte was downright suspicious of me. And curious, too, about what I was telling. One day when I was out in the orchard helping Father, she rummaged around in my room. When I got back to the house, I was greeted with a dead silence. I knew then that the notes had been read, even though they were in exactly the same spot where I had left them.

"Supper ready soon?" I asked humbly.

"*We* are having supper later," said Charlotte pointedly.

Aunt Rachel deliberately turned her back on me and looked out of the window. The storm would break at any moment now. I felt that I had better get out while the going was good.

If my ambitions to act upon the stage had been frustrated, I could try acting off the stage. So, in the best manner of the noble hero in *No Mother to Guide Her*, I said melodramatically, "I have a feeling I'm not welcome around here."

"How right you are!" said Charlotte.

Putting on my hat, coat, and rubbers, I murmured "Good-by, a long good-by." Then I walked across the snow-covered fields to town and went to the early show at the movies—and that gave me an idea.

When I got back, Charlotte was entertaining one of her goggling beaux in the living room. Aunt Rachel, seated by the stove, was grimly knitting.

Mother said, "I've kept your supper hot for you in the oven, Carl."

I sat down at the table in the kitchen, and as she served me she said, soberly, "Your spelling is atrocious, and now and then you have awkward sentences. Every once in a while you try to be cute. But on the whole I think maybe you have some talent as a writer. I've been able to identify most of the people you are writing about. But some of the descriptions aren't nearly as amusing as you intended them to be."

Father came in with a bottle of bourbon. "Join me?" he asked. "You were sort of rough on us, Carl, and I'm wondering if it's a good idea for you to write a play about all of us here in the Bitter

Root. Suppose it should get produced? We'd be in a tough spot. We've got to live here and keep as many friends as possible."

I agreed with Father on that score. And besides writing a full-length play would take an awful lot of time. Why not try and make some quick money? The movies I had seen that night had stirred my imagination. Why shouldn't I try my hand at writing a scenario? According to the movie magazines, the picture companies were willing to pay real money for an acceptable scenario. And one even said they'd go as high as $25 for an original script.

This was in the days of the one- and two-reel silent pictures. The stories were short and to the point. So I began to write scenarios. I didn't tell the family what I was doing. They hadn't liked my idea for a play. How would they feel about movie stories? They certainly weren't literature—and not even art. I mailed them out as fast as I could. They all bounced back.

Naturally the family became curious as to what was in the large self-addressed envelopes. Was I touched in the head, and writing letters to myself? When I ultimately had to tell them the truth, Father thought it was all nonsense. Why didn't I go into town like a young, ambitious man should and get myself a job of some sort? He considered it complete insanity on my part to shut myself up in my room day after day and write stories that invariably were returned.

"It's not good business," he said. "Suppose I manufactured engines that nobody wanted and were always sent back? I'd soon do something else—and damned fast. It's pure foolishness—and I don't see why you waste your time this way."

My sister began to call me "Shakespeare."

It got to the point where, not to let the family know, I'd be the one to collect the mail. The thick envelopes I'd hide. I didn't have any money, of course. But Mother would sneak me some change now and then for postage. And Father—who was trying to discipline me—would pay me when I neglected my writing and helped him about the ranch.

Then one morning came a letter—a long, thin letter—the most glorious letter that a writer can receive. When I got back to the house, I was asked, "Any more rejected manuscripts this morning?"

"I don't remember," I answered casually.

But at lunch I sprang my surprise.

"I'd like to invite all of you to have dinner in town with me next Saturday," I said, "and then we'll go to the movies afterwards."

"Who'll pay for it?" asked Father. "Me?"

I took my time. Slowly bringing forth the letter, I handed it to Father, without saying a word. He read it aloud. It was an acceptance of one of my scenarios, and enclosed was a check for the munificent sum of $25!

"I'll be damned!" said Father. "I didn't think it possible."

"I knew it all the time," said Mother, as she kissed me and wiped a tear from her eyes.

From that moment the family ate out of my hand, and the world was my oyster. Aunt Rachel forgot all about my disgraceful behavior as an actor and what I had said about her first drink, and now insisted on sharpening my pencils daily. Even Charlotte was a trifle overcome. The only thing any of her beaux had ever written were love letters. Those I read when she wasn't around, while not publishable, still did contain some good material, which I used in my own way. The scenario that I had sold was entitled *Modern Love* and was based on my observations of Charlotte and her beaux. But I had so changed the locale and so disguised the various characters that I don't think they would have recognized themselves.

"It will be a proud moment for your Mother and me when we see one of your stories on the screen," said Father. "I'll spread the manure on the orchard—you keep on writing!"

"It's really wonderful that you're now a writer," said Mother. "I'm so glad for you. A writer has such an exciting life. You'll meet such interesting people and make so many fine friends. And both your Father and I think you must go back to college next winter."

But just how this could be managed was a problem. There were no profits from the apple orchard. In fact, the ranch was still losing money, and the family savings were almost gone. If I went back to college, it meant that I must earn my own way. But that, I felt, would be easy. I'd pay all my expenses by writing movie scenarios.

However, Father suggested that I'd better get myself some kind of a job to fall back upon, as perhaps writing might prove a little uncertain. He was right. I wrote some fifteen more scenarios before I made another sale.

Going back to Northwestern was out of the question. It was too far away, too expensive, and the family felt I might meet up again with bad companions, like Sylvia, who would lead me astray. If I went to the State University at Missoula, not many miles away, I'd meet only nice people and make a really honest penny.

6

WE NEVER WERE WARMER

AT THAT time, over thirty years ago, Missoula was a wide-open, breezy, friendly, yet gun-toting typical Western town. At the far end of the town, nestled against the foot of the mountains—serene, sedate, and aloof—was the campus of the State University. Downtown, a block from the main thoroughfare of the business section, was the red-light district.

Here were the saloons, the cribs, and the parlor houses. In the parlor houses were the best of the career girls, under the chaperonage of a madame. On pay day at Fort Missoula the soldiers made a beeline for Front Street. And on Saturday nights, when the lumberjacks and miners were in town, the red-light district was crowded.

One Saturday night a few of us, being curious and fortified by a few drinks to give us courage, left the campus and began a tour of Front Street. We rang the bell of Gussie's establishment, the most select and best known of the parlor houses. A well-groomed maid let us in. Gussie herself came to greet us in the parlor.

She was a woman somewhere in her forties, with red hair. In her hair she stuck incense sticks, and lighted them. As she moved about, she resembled a flaming Medusa. She was a handsome woman and wore an evening gown with grace and distinction. That evening when she saw us, she groaned.

"College boys!" she said, and shuddered. Then she added, politely but sternly, "Now sit down and behave yourselves. But look—why do you have to come around on my very busiest night? You haven't any money to spend in the first place—and the town's full of lumberjacks with fat bank rolls. This may be a pleasure house—but what's pleasure to you is business to me. You can have one glass of beer, and then you've got to go!"

The beer, a very short glass, cost fifty cents. Out of an ordinary bottle costing ten cents, in those days, Gussie could retail some six glasses. We sat down stiffly and as ill at ease as if we were at a reception being given by the Dean of Women. At one end of the tiny dance hall was a piano.

"Mind if I play something?" I asked.

"If you don't play too loud!" said Gussie. "And no dance music, because the girls would think I wanted them in the parlor—which I don't."

I played one of my favorite numbers, "Rustle of Spring."

"That's lovely," murmured Gussie. "Play some more."

I played "The End of a Perfect Day," and with flourishes concluded with that sentimental song, "The Rosary."

When I finished, Gussie had tears in her eyes. "That's awfully sweet. I love that song. It's one of my favorites. Now if you'll be good boys and run along back to school, I'll let you come some week night and play for me again. Maybe some of my girls would like to hear you play, too."

"Yes, ma'am. Thank you, ma'am," we said politely, and went our way.

Often I'd see Gussie walking down the main business street. She was the smartest dressed woman in town, as she'd go quietly about her shopping, looking neither to right or left. Nobody spoke to her.

She spoke to nobody. But Gussie was a rich woman. The town's bank had a huge glass window on a corner. Now and then Gussie could be seen seated primly in the chair at the window, talking to the bank's president, who advised her on investments.

But her financial standing and mine were miles apart. I did all sorts of odd jobs—piled wood in basements for twenty-five cents an hour, tended babies now and then, and helped with house-cleaning and other honest chores. It just about paid my board and room, and I didn't have enough money left over to go to the theater often.

For Missoula was a great show town. It served as a stopover for traveling companies between Spokane and Butte, and all the great stars of the day played in Missoula: Otis Skinner, John Drew, Blanche Ring, Walker Whiteside, and others. Now and then, on a busy Saturday, I jerked soda for a candy store run by an amiable Greek. One night I was complaining about how I wanted to see a show but didn't have enough money.

"I got an idea," he said. "Let's talk to the manager of the theater. Maybe he'll let you sell candy between the acts. Give him a cut, if necessary. He'll make money. I'll make money. You'll make money and get to see the show free."

So it was arranged. But what a comedown for a former Shakespearean star! Here I was, at twenty-one, ending a career in the theater doing what most famous actors did at the beginning—selling candy during intermissions!

Whenever a great star appeared, it was always a gala event. The whole town turned out. The officers from Fort Missoula, in their full-dress uniforms, would occupy the boxes with their wives. The faculty and the society leaders, in their best bib and tucker, would sit in style in the orchestra. But the choicest seats in the house, the third and fourth row, were always taken by Gussie and her girls. They'd arrive early in a body, take their seats quietly and modestly, laugh at the jokes in a restrained manner, and shed a sentimental tear at the sad moments. While they did not exactly overdress, still there was no question that they were the best-gowned women in the audience.

I soon found that selling candy to the local Four Hundred was impossible. The only customers I had in the orchestra were Gussie's girls. Just as soon as they were seated, I'd start up the aisle, crying "Candy and peanuts!" The girls would reach into their purses, and every single one would buy a box of chocolates. They loved sweets.

When my tray was empty, I'd dash back to the candy store, stock up on ten-cent bags of candy, and then start my rounds of the balcony and gallery, which contained my next best customers.

It wasn't long until I got another steady job. The Reverend Mr. Gatley, Rector of the Episcopal Church, was a good friend. He offered me the job of janitor at the church—or "sexton," as it was then called. This meant that on Saturdays I'd scrub and clean the church, and dust the cushions. Then early on Sunday mornings, around eight o'clock, I'd start the fires, so that the church would be warm in time for services.

Thus I was kept busy—what with the work I had to do to pay my expenses, and my studies at the University. I didn't have the time or the money for social activities on the campus. I was often lonely. I read everything assigned to me in my English courses— and more. I soon found that the naughty ladies were much more fascinating to read about than the conventional good women. Becky Sharp in *Vanity Fair* was a much more exciting person than plain, drab Amelia. Camille was no angel, either, nor were Carmen, Nana, Anna Karenina, and many others. They lived, they sinned, they repented and suffered—but oh, how thrilling were their stories, and damned good reading, too.

One particular night when the library was closed, I didn't know what to do with myself. Then I remembered what Gussie had said about coming and playing for her. Someday, perhaps, I might want to write a novel about a naughty heroine. Here was a golden opportunity to actually become acquainted with one.

I grabbed a handful of music, went down to Front Street, and rang the doorbell. It was a quiet weekday night, and customers were few and far between. Gussie, when she saw the music under my arm, let me in. I played for her. She even opened a bottle of beer for me, and wouldn't let me pay for it. That was the beginning of my friendship with Gussie.

At first, of course, I didn't ask any questions about her life. I thought that perhaps she would tell me about herself, but she didn't. Finally my curiosity got the better of me, and I was impertinent enough to inquire as to how she got started in her present business.

"Look," she said (but she wasn't as mad as she should have been), "that's a question every damn man asks. And I've got a different answer for every damn one of them. How does anybody go into business? Why does one man became a banker, another a lawyer, another a storekeeper? They got to make a living, don't they? Same with me. How I got started is none of your damn business, and don't go asking me that silly question again."

But of course I told Gussie all about myself, and how, now that my ambitions to become an actor had come to an untimely end, I was planning to become a writer.

"I love books," I said, "and someday I want to write the great American novel."

"I bet you will, too," she said. "You're just enough of a damn fool to do something like that. But keep up your education, boy. What you studying over there at the University?"

I told her the courses I was taking, and the books I was reading.

"Look," she said, "the next time you come, bring me some of those books to read. I'm curious about what they're putting into the minds of young people these days. . . . I used to read a lot when I was young. But I've been much too busy lately—and I think a lady should be properly educated."

So I took Gussie all the required reading I was doing in courses in English Literature: Wordsworth, Shelley, Keats, and all the poets; also all the novels by the great writers. I would even, now and then, bring along my lecture notes and go over them with her. It was a good review for me, and an excellent liberal arts education for Gussie. She became an avid reader, and I carried away from the library more books than any other student. It impressed the librarian no end, and pleased my English professors immensely.

One Thursday night when I visited Gussie after library hours, she said, "Look, I'm in a dilemma." She was discovering new and big words, and using them correctly, too. "My professor is ill."

"You mean your other professor," I said jokingly.

"I do," she replied soberly.

(To those whose innocent past does not embrace the wide-open days of thirty years ago, it must be explained that there used to be two kinds of "professors." One kind taught in schools and colleges, and did so quite openly. Then there was another kind of professor—the piano player in establishments such as Gussie's.)

Her professor was an indefinite, nebulous, thoroughly undistinguished, seedy individual. He sat at the piano, a green shade over his eyes, a cigarette dangling from his lips; and when Gussie would cry out, "Gentlemen in the parlor, girls," he'd bang out dance music like an automaton.

"Now he's ill," said Gussie. "He just doesn't take care of his health. And this Saturday is going to be a big night—convention in town, and lots of lumberjacks, too. Now, look—will you do me a favor?"

"Hm," I replied, hesitatingly, as I knew exactly what she was going to suggest.

"It'll be for only a couple of Saturdays at the most. And when anybody buys a round, the professor always gets a beer, too. This is the way we work it. I keep half on every glass the girls sell—the other half is theirs. The professor always gets his cut as well. On top of that, I'll pay you a dollar an hour out of my own pocket.

"Sometimes, figuring in the liquor money, the professor gets as much as twenty or twenty-five dollars a night. All our customers will be strangers in town—you'll wear a green shade, and who will know you? You'll be needing money for tuition next semester—and you need a new suit of clothes right now. What's the answer?"

So for three Saturday nights I played the piano for my friend Gussie, and was glad that I had the chance to do her a favor. The hours were long, but nobody paid the slightest attention to me.

Gussie advised me not to drink all the beers offered me, as I might get tight. In the corner by the piano was a spittoon, and when no one was looking, instead of down the hatch, into the spittoon went my beer.

Around five o'clock or so in the morning, when the last guest had departed, Gussie and all the girls would gather in the dining room at the back for their midnight supper. The most popular dish was raw hamburgers with plenty of onions. As the girls sat around the table they'd swap yarns of their adventures. Listening to them talk was, for me, a liberal education. Here was plenty of material for the great American novel, for their stories had everything: tears and laughter, success and failure, and plenty of human interest.

When I'd had my supper, I'd take off the green shade and walk through the silent streets to the church, where I'd start the fires. Getting them going at six o'clock instead of eight made the church delightfully warm and comfortable by the time the service was ready to start.

I was highly complimented by some of the ladies in the church, those three Sundays. "You're the best sexton we've ever had," they said. "We've never been warmer."

Constant attendance at all the services was beginning to have an effect on me. I had never been baptized. I had never joined a church. I could easily become an Episcopalian with no sins—save those of heresy—to be forgiven. And I found the services beautiful and comforting. So I joined the Episcopal Church, was properly baptized, and felt very happy. My godmother was a devoted church worker, a sincere, genuine, understanding, and lovable person, and one of the best cooks I've ever known.

She lived with her husband and family in a quiet neighborhood where the rows of houses were so close that you could practically shake hands with your neighbor over the back fence. One day there moved into the house next door a man and his wife. My godmother, being a friendly person, went one afternoon to call and welcome the newcomers to the neighborhood. But she had a strange reception.

When she rapped upon the door, the wife unlocked it, opened it a bit, and said, "Yes?"

"I've come to welcome you to Missoula," said my godmother.

"I gather you are a stranger in town—and I want to be neighborly."

"Thank you kindly," said the woman. "But we won't be here long. I'd ask you in, but my husband is ill this afternoon. Thank you, and good afternoon."

It was a complete brush-off, something which had never happened to my godmother before. She was quite upset about it.

"It's the strangest thing," she said. "She's a fine-looking woman, too—but she wouldn't let me in. I can't understand it."

None of us could. Then one evening when I was having dinner with my godmother and her family, I went out to the back porch to get the ice cream for dessert. The next-door neighbor was also on the back porch. I stared in astonishment. It was Gussie!

She put her finger on her lips, cautioning me to be silent, and whispered, "Come see me—when you can."

Shortly after dinner I excused myself, saying that I had some studying to do. I walked around the block, came back, and rapped on Gussie's door. She let me in. Her red hair was done up neatly and becomingly—and there were no incense sticks.

"I'm married," said Gussie. "Come and meet my husband."

He was seated in the living room, reading the paper.

"Fred," said Gussie, "this is my professor from the University. You've heard me speak of him."

Fred greeted me pleasantly and asked me to sit down, and would I like a highball? He was a sort of shriveled-up little man with a too-black mustache and pale, watery eyes.

Gussie patted him affectionately, and said, "Fred may not be much to look at, but he's sure kind to me."

"Quit your kidding," responded Fred, giving Gussie a loving pinch.

Then Gussie told me what had happened. She had sold her business.

"Got a good price, too," she said. "And Fred's been saving for years. He's got a bank roll almost the size of mine. He owned a gambling joint over in Butte. So we decided to get married and retire. We're going some place where nobody knows us—and settle down for a comfortable old age together. We're neither of us spring chickens, and might as well take it easy for what years we've got left. And there's an awful lot of reading I want to get caught up on."

"Gussie's been having me read some of those books you've recommended," said Fred. "Not bad—some of them. Not at all bad."

"And, one of these days when we get our own home, I'm going to have a hell of a fine library, too," said Gussie. "Thanks to you, Prof."

Before I left that night I told Gussie about my godmother next door, and said that I had joined a church.

"That's a good thing," said Gussie. "Fred was raised a Baptist. I guess one of these days I'll join a church, too. It won't hurt me none— I'm awfully sorry about being so rude to your friend next door, but what else could I do? She'd ask me a lot of questions, and I'm damned sick and tired of telling lies. Anyway, ladies like her don't want to know ladies like me. Not right away, anyway. Not until I've made good in their way of life."

Not long after, Gussie and her husband moved away. But I was to hear from her once in a while in the years to come. Now and then I'd get a letter with nothing in the envelope but a newspaper clipping. Summed up, they showed Gussie's rise in the world: how Mr. and Mrs. Blank, retired farmers from Pennsylvania, had purchased a new home; how Mrs. Blank had joined the woman's club and would review some of the latest books at the next meeting; how Mrs. Blank had entertained the sewing circle of the church and delicious refreshments were served; and so forth, and so forth.

All this was long ago, and much has happened since then. But I've always been sorry that Gussie passed away before my first book was published. I know that she would have given it a fine and glowing review for the literary section of her woman's club.

❧❧

7

HAIL AND FAREWELL

When I started writing this book, I dropped a note to Dr. George F. Reynolds and told him what I was doing. He was Professor of English during those years that I attended the University of Montana. He replied to my letter, saying, "It's always been a fear of mine that some student would get me into a book. It's dangerous to know writers! But go ahead. As to some of the stories you say you are planning to tell, what can I add, and what should I know, innocent that I am."

He hasn't changed a bit in all the years that I have known him: still modest, encouraging, paradoxical, and disarming. And he doesn't really mean that it's dangerous to know writers. Unlike many dreary-eyed, bored professors who look upon their students as necessary evils, George Reynolds loved his students and was particularly fond of embryonic, half-baked, aspiring young writers. Of all the teachers I knew in my college days, he was the most helpful and inspiring at a time when I most needed help and encouragement. And ever since, I have always looked upon Dr. Reynolds in the approved Chinese style as my Number One Teacher.

Every session of every class was to him a fresh adventure. He'd come bouncing into the classroom with all the suppressed enthusiasm of a circus horse smelling the sawdust. He'd lecture with a sparkle in his eye, and so conceal his profound scholarship that he'd make even Aristotle's *Poetics* seem palatable. He'd scold us and praise us; but he praised more often than he scolded. And so genuine was his love of literature and the art of writing that it was impossible not to share his enthusiasms.

When I told him I wanted to become a writer, he hemmed and hawed a bit and wanted to know what I was writing. My scenarios in those days were all faint echoes of the threadbare plots I was seeing on the screen. I wrote stories of life in wicked New York City, where I had never been. My characters were sinful multimillionaires, whose selfish seeking of pleasure brought sorrow to suffering shop-girls. I also wrote tragic tales of debauchery among the wild-eyed Bohemian artists who drowned their sorrows in drink or vice versa. None of these scenarios sold. They were all returned to me with the comment, "Not true to life."

"Why don't you write about people you know," suggested Dr. Reynolds.

"But I know only good people, and they never do anything," I replied. Then I pompously expounded my theory that, while good people were nice to know and made fine, loyal friends, still their stories made damned poor reading. The solid, substantial cousin who could always be depended upon to take over in times of family stress was pretty often a very dull chap. The cousin whom we discussed most often in the family circles was the black sheep—and if I wrote him up, he'd be sore.

Then I also told Dr. Reynolds my theory of the fascination of the scarlet ladies in literature, and, going a step further, said that the Robin Hoods, the Falstaffs, and the scamps and the scoundrels were by far the most interesting.

"Shocking, of course. Shocking!" replied Dr. Reynolds, with a twinkle in his eye. "But I'm afraid that's very true. If everybody in this world was good, there'd be nothing to write about, I grant you. But there's plenty of drama and conflict to be found when a good person comes in contact with someone evil. Why not use that thought as a springboard, and go on from there?"

It was an excellent point, and cleared up my muddled thinking. Into the wastepaper basket went the stories of the too-wicked millionaires and the too-virtuous shopgirls. I also read, somewhere or other, that the combination of sex and religion never failed. And so, from the sound advice given me by Dr. Reynolds, I thought up the story of a good man.

It was a simple story, and, frankly, a trifle corny. My hero was an old man who took into his home, when others had cast her out, a young mother with a baby and no husband! His action raised quite a disturbance in the community, and even the preacher strongly objected. But the old man, whose name was Peter, took down his shotgun when he discovered who the father was, and marched the young man and the unwed mother straight to the door of the preacher's home. And the young man? Who was he? That's right—the preacher's only son!

But the story was accepted by the American Film Company, and the editor, Thomas Rickets, wrote me, asking for more scenarios along that line. When it was finally produced, it was entitled *Unto the Weak*, and the advertisements all said, "A powerful sociological drama of moral regeneration, teeming with pathos and tense situations."

From then on, all the scenarios I wrote dealt in a big way with "moral regeneration" of one sort or another—and the damn things sold.

At home on a week end I read the story of *Unto the Weak* aloud to the family.

Aunt Rachel said, "I don't see where you get ideas like that. I don't think it's true to life. All the preacher's sons I've ever known were exactly like their fathers."

Father gave me a wink and murmured, "What this world needs is better and bigger shotgun weddings."

My sister, who by this time was married to a promising young attorney in Hamilton, wanted to know why I didn't write a story about a naive girl who fell in love, and said, "Not a single one of my friends has ever even had a premature baby."

Still, on the whole the family approved the high moral tone of my story. And Father said that, when the scenario was produced, he'd give a theater party, invite all their friends, and applaud loudly, even if people didn't usually applaud at the movies.

But the next winter Mother became seriously ill. The doctor told Father that he should take her to a lower altitude. Quickly Father came to a decision. Being a gentleman rancher had not proved a successful venture. He again advertised the ranch for sale, and auctioned off all the furniture, the books, everything. The house was stripped bare.

So back to Marshalltown went Father and Mother. Father was fifty-nine, no longer a young man. But he still had the spirit and grit of his pioneer forefathers. His savings of years had melted away in the Bitter Root. He had no capital to invest and start a new business. He took the first job at hand, that of shipping clerk in a factory now owned by one of his former foremen. He held his head high, never complained, and carried on as best he could under the circumstances.

In the old days all the workers in his factory had called him by his first name. Many of his former employees, with whom he was now working side by side, still called him "Charlie." That pleased Father and made him very proud. He wrote me, saying that while he was poor in dollars he was rich in friends.

In the meantime *Unto the Weak* was released, the first of my scenarios to be produced. It was announced to be shown in Marshalltown on January 28. Father was delighted. He practically bought out the entire house for the first showing, and invited all our relatives and his friends. I'm certain he couldn't quite afford it, but somehow or other he was going to manage.

There was a story in the Missoula paper, announcing the showing of the play there, too; but the story concluded by saying, "Carl Glick will not be in Missoula to see his play produced here, having been called to his former home in Iowa by the death of his father."

Father passed away very suddenly, of pneumonia, a week before the theater party he had planned. On the day of his funeral all the factories in town were closed, and his co-workers filled the church. And so passed from the scene the best friend I had ever had. He was a good Joe, my Dad.

I went alone to the theater when *Unto the Weak* was shown. But there was no joy in it for me, no thrill, and no fulfillment. Sad and unhappy, I went to the hospital and told Mother about it.

"Your Father was very proud, Carl—pleased and happy—knowing it was to be. He's glad that you have decided to be a writer— as I am. But promise me one thing—don't ever, if you can help it, write anything that will hurt anybody. That would have made your Father unhappy. He was always kindly, gentle, and friendly, and liked people—as I hope you do, too."

Then she gave me the diamond engagement ring from her finger, which Father had given her, and asked me to keep it for the girl that someday I would marry. The next day Mother passed away.

I had one more year of college. I could, of course, have returned to Montana, but it seemed so far away. In Chicago, not far from Northwestern University, were the headquarters of some of the picture companies for whom I was writing scenarios. I felt that being on the ground would be of help. And when Father's estate was settled, I found that, if I lived modestly, I would not have to work my way through my senior year. That would give me more time for my writing. So back to Northwestern I went.

During my senior year there, one of my favorite restaurants in Chicago was a small French table d'hôte, an out-of-the-way spot where for fifty cents you'd get a dinner that was tops, with a bottle of red wine thrown in for good measure. It was quite famous among Chicago's artistic Bohemian crowd, and the local celebrities who dined there were thicker than fleas. It was located in the basement of a gloomy old house on Federal Court, just outside the Loop. Once upon a time it had been a notorious bawdy house, and one of the sights upstairs was the room with mirrors.

But now it was owned by a jovial, diminutive Frenchwoman, Madame Ackerman. She was a rolypoly old lady with a huge middle-aged stomach, and she waddled as she walked. She ran the upstairs part as a boarding house for waiters and had her own restaurant in the basement, which she conducted to suit herself— and if you didn't like it you could go elsewhere, thank you. There were only two small rooms. In the front room was a large table where everybody sat, family style. In the back room were smaller tables. Dinner was at seven o'clock. Madame Ackerman would wait patiently until every seat was taken, then she'd lock the door, and dinner would be served as if everybody was a guest in her home.

When you dined at Madame Ackerman's, you went expecting to stay the entire evening. The best fun was after dinner. Anybody who had a parlor trick up his sleeve performed. Those who could sing a song, sang. Those who could tell a story, told it. Everybody talked to everyone else. It was glorious fun, having dinner at Madame Ackerman's. If you put sugar into the sour red wine, it increased the alcoholic content—and that always helped loosen tongues and liven things up.

The French consul in Chicago had a small table in the back room reserved for him. Occasionally he would bring along a guest. One evening he had with him a most attractive woman, rather plainly dressed. They chatted like magpies in French, and toasted each other every other minute. After dinner, when the stunts began, someone asked her, "What can you do?"

"I sing a little," she said modestly.

"I play a little," I exclaimed. "Come on—let's go."

I sat down at the piano. On the music rack were some of the popular songs of the day. I played, and the guest of the French consul sang. And how she sang! She fairly took the roof off. Everyone cheered and applauded.

Being an impertinent young college squirt and thinking I was funny, I said, "Sister—you've got a wonderful voice. You should do something with it. You have talent. You should take lessons!"

"Oh-la-la," she smiled. "You sweet little boy!"

She patted me on the head and then made a dramatic exit to our thunderous applause. But Madame Ackerman was having hysterics.

"Mon dieu—mon dieu," she moaned. "That was Madame Emma Calvé, the great opera star!"

I had to borrow money from my friends—because drinks for everyone present were on me.

When I wrote about this to my former music teacher in Marshall-town, Ralph Hix, he replied, "Congratulations. Playing accompaniments for the great Calvé is a goal I never dreamed you would some day attain. Incidentally, what are you going to do after you graduate?"

I didn't know. I would have liked to support myself by writing—but the sales were too few and far between. I presumed I'd have to get myself some sort of a job. Then came a latter from Ralph Hix, saying that he had been appointed Dean of the Conservatory of Music at Fairmount College in Wichita, Kansas, and wanted someone to teach dramatic art. Would I be interested? I definitely was. I had never taught dramatic art and knew nothing whatsoever about it. But I had been in college plays, as well as in repertory and on the road, and had even taken a fling at directing. So why couldn't I do what a lot of other teachers did—learn while teaching?

Fairmount College was a small Congregational Church school. The president, on one of his trips to Chicago, interviewed me. He warned me that dancing, card playing, and smoking were not allowed at Fairmount. But that didn't bother me, as I didn't care too much for dancing or card playing anyway. However, giving plays was perfectly all right, as that was considered a cultural activity, and stimulating intellectually. Teaching would give me plenty of time on the side, too, to go on with my writing. And being a faculty member in a small church school would be an entirely new experience for me.

So, the September after graduation from Northwestern, off I went to Wichita, Kansas. I was determined to behave properly, to do in Rome as the Romans did, and to be as good a professor as possible. But, as usual, upon arriving at Fairmount College, I immediately got off on the wrong foot.

8

WILD CHERRY PHOSPHATE

FAIRMOUNT COLLEGE was at the edge of town, high on a hill overlooking Wichita, and surrounded on three sides by cornfields. I arrived three days before registration, so when I got off the streetcar at the end of the line, lugging my suitcase, the campus was deserted. I had been told I was to live in the men's dormitory—which was easy to find, as the other two buildings were obviously the Main Hall and the Library.

There was only one person around: an elderly man clad in overalls and an old sweater. He was busy sweeping the halls, and so I took it for granted that he was the janitor. I introduced myself.

"We've been expecting you," he said.

Then he showed me where my room was to be. I handed him fifty cents and asked that he please see that my trunk was sent up from the station.

But he handed the fifty cents back to me, saying, "I'm not the janitor. I'm Professor of Biblical Literature. We all give a helping hand with the work around here. This is a Christian college."

So I grabbed a broom, too, and began to sweep out my room. It was plain and unadorned, with walls badly in need of a coat of paint, no curtains at the windows, and a dilapidated iron cot that sagged in the middle. And I was warned by the Professor of Biblical

Literature not to open my windows too wide when the wind blew—
as it frequently did—for the dust storms got things pretty dirty.

When the students arrived, I learned that a great number of them
were studying for the ministry. There were some, however, who were
merely seeking an education. And of course they all went to church
regularly, both morning and evening services. It was on a Sunday
shortly after registration that I made my second error.

On Sunday evenings all the students went over to town to church.
I went to town, too—but not to church. On this particular Sunday
I rambled around by myself, wondering what to find by way of
amusement. There wasn't any. Down by the railway station I
dropped into a soda fountain. I remembered how, back in Marshalltown, Aunt America used to treat me occasionally at Uncle Cliff's
drugstore. So I asked for what had been at that time one of my
favorite soft drinks, a wild cherry phosphate. I started sipping it
through a straw. It was a mighty funny-tasting wild cherry phosphate. I threw away the straw and took a big drink. My worst sus-
picions were confirmed.

"What's this I got here?" I said to the soda jerker.

"You asked for a wild cherry phosphate, didn't you," he said
with a sly wink. "Well—that's what you got!"

"Thanks, pal," I said happily. "Let's have another—double."

Since they allowed more than one to a customer, I poured them
down as fast as I could. I think I must have overdone it a bit, for I
was in a fine glow as I staggered out to catch the streetcar back to
Fairmount College.

Services at the church were over, and the car was crowded with
students. The only vacant seat was away up in front, facing everybody in the car. The world was good, everybody was my friend, and
I was in fine fettle. As I made my way to the seat, I spoke to all the

students, individually and collectively. I slapped them on the back, said "Hi, there!" and "How's tricks?" Finding my seat, I went into a sort of monologue, telling them what a wonderful thing higher education was and how I hoped that they were all going to make the most of their opportunities.

They smiled happily and said they "sure would."

The next morning the Dean of Women asked me to drop into her office for a moment. She greeted me with a friendly smile. "I have a compliment for you, Professor Glick," she said. "Some of the students have told me how you rode out on the streetcar with them last evening."

"Yes, ma'am," I said, soberly.

"They seem to think you are an awfully jolly fellow, and I'm so glad you are fitting so well into our happy family life here at Fairmount."

"Yes, ma'am," I said. "I'm trying."

"But it's not too difficult?" she said, anxiously.

"No, ma'am—not at all."

"I do hope you'll be popular here with the students, but I do want to warn you about one thing!"

I held my breath. Now it was coming.

"You aren't really too much older than some of our seniors here —and while, of course, the faculty always likes to have the students look upon us as their best friends, still we must set them a good example. And so, if you don't mind my advising you—it's best not, for the sake of discipline, to mingle too freely with the students. We have very happy times at our faculty parties, and I'm certain you will find our society very stimulating."

"Yes, ma'am," I said.

So I went to the faculty parties. We always played games of one sort or another. One professor had a box full of puzzles, which we all tried diligently to solve. At another professor's home, amidst gales of laughter, we'd be blindfolded and then try to pin the tail on the donkey's rear. It was all such good-natured fun. The parties, however, all broke up early. And then I'd make my lonely way over to town and have a wild cherry phosphate before going to bed. I found that drink very relaxing after a hilarious evening.

The entire faculty and student body were expected to attend chapel every morning. I was most regular in attendance, and sang the hymns as loudly and as lustily as the best of the theological students. I was trying hard to be on good behavior. And then I stuck my neck out again.

Quite a number of my scenarios had been produced by this time, and why not have them shown downtown at one of the movie theaters? I spoke to Mr. Fox, the manager of one of the theaters, and a deal was made. He would show my highly "moral and educational" scenarios about regeneration. It was arranged that, for every ticket sold to the students at Fairmount, 25 percent would go to the Fairmount Athletic Association, and once a week there would be a "Fairmount Night" at the theater.

Came the evening of the opening of the season. Some of the students had hung the lobby with Fairmount banners, and it was to be a gala event. A large crowd was on hand, including several members of the faculty. I arrived at the theater early, and Mr. Fox called me hurriedly to one side.

"Migawd!" he said. "Here we're sold out—have advertised your play—and the damned distributors in Kansas City have sent us the wrong film. It isn't your story at all. What shall we do?"

"Damned if I know!" I said.

Yet the show, we both felt, must go on.

"Look," whispered Mr. Fox, with the air of an arch-conspirator. "What say we show the picture we got—and say nothing? What the hell—nobody will know the difference! If we let them down on the first picture, nobody will come the second time."

It made sense. "Go ahead," I said.

I took my seat. Fox had prepared a slide announcing that the next picture was one written by Professor Carl Glick of the faculty of Fairmount College, and that other pictures of his writing would be shown regularly. When the slide flashed on the screen, everyone applauded vigorously. Then the picture began to flicker on the screen. Instead of my story *The Test of Truth*, it was an enticing little number called *The Troublesome Wink*.

And it was troublesome. It was a slapstick comedy of the old days of silent pictures. There was a gal in a bathing suit who had an eye affliction and simply couldn't help winking. As she walked innocently along the beach, she winked, and winked, and winked. Men everywhere rose and followed her—for her wink was of that sort. She began to run, still winking. More men joined in the chase. The Keystone cops took over, and—

But by that time I had practically sunk out of sight in my seat and was wondering how I could crawl out of the theater on my hands and knees without being seen. When the picture came to an end, the audience sighed—but no one applauded.

I managed to escape unharmed from the theater, and hurried to the soda fountain.

"Wild cherry phosphate, please," I said to the soda jerker.

"Okay, pal," he replied—and winked!

The next morning, on my way to chapel as usual, the president stopped me.

"We were all a trifle disappointed by your literary effort as shown on the screen at the theater last evening," he said grimly.

There was but one thing for me to do, tell him the truth. I said that I thought it was a good joke on me, but he didn't quite see it that way. He suggested, kindly and authoritatively, that perhaps an explanation had better be made to the faculty and students. So at chapel that morning, after the opening hymn had been sung and the prayer made, I publicly confessed. I promised that, the next time one of my pictures was to be shown, I'd see it first and be certain that it was something of my own authorship. Then I waxed highly moral, and delivered them a short sermon against the sin of admitting to doing something they hadn't actually done.

But not long after this unfortunate episode I was forgiven by the faculty, because of a prayer I made in faculty meeting. This meeting was especially called one afternoon, because of one of the most disgraceful scandals ever known to have occurred on the fair campus of Fairmount College.

One evening I was going through the hall of the dormitory on my way to my room, when I ran into a student. George had just returned from Kansas City, where he had been a delegate to the Y.M.C.A. Conference. I asked him if he had had an inspiring time. He replied that he had.

"It was both inspiring—and stimulating," he said, and grinned a trifle foolishly.

I understood what he meant, for to my horror I smelled liquor on his breath.

"You've been drinking," I whispered.

"Right you are, Professor," he whispered back. "After seeing your masterpiece *The Troublesome Wink*, I hope you aren't shocked."

"Properly so," I replied.

Then, being young and boastful, he told me the whole story. He had brought back with him from Kansas City a bottle of Angelica wine. And even at that very moment, upstairs in his room several of the boys were taking turns sipping from the bottle.

"Come and join us," he said. I presume he thought that if he could involve a faculty member, everything would be all right. But I knew that if I did drink, I'd be blackmailed for the rest of my stay at Fairmount. So, nobly, I declined, saying that I didn't drink Angelica wine.

"Don't tell me you object to liquor," he sneered. "I bet you know where to get it right here in Wichita, too. You were pretty unsteady on your feet that night you got on the streetcar. Gave some of us food for thought. How about it?"

"Relax," I said. "I don't object. But if you want a drink, why don't you have a real one—like whisky. Why Angelica wine?"

"Whisky? That's strong stuff—and I couldn't afford it. Whisky! You shock me, Professor. Is that what you drink?" He leered.

"Forget about it!" I leered back, and tried hard to make it appear that my feelings had been hurt.

"Okay, Professor," he grinned. "Sure you won't join us?"

"Positive—thanks just the same," I replied.

He went back to the brawl upstairs, where, we later learned, some eight students thought they got awfully drunk on a single bottle of mild Angelica wine.

But there was one lad who wasn't invited, and that made him sore. The next morning he told what had gone on, most confidentially to his girl, who told it confidentially to the Dean of Women, who told it confidentially to the president, who told it confidentially to the Dean of Men, who told it confidentially to one of the professors, who told it confidentially to his wife, who immediately got on the phone and told it confidentially to several other faculty wives, and by noon the whole campus knew about it. The story spread over town, and the episode took on varied sinister meanings. By evening the affair had reached the proportions of a national calamity.

The next morning a newspaper reporter telephoned the president. He had to hurry over town to see the editor and beg for the suppression of the scandal. The rival college in town, another small church school, heard about it. They were almost considering canceling the big football game of the year. They certainly wouldn't pit their strength and purity against the drunkards at Fairmount College.

All day long, classes were practically suspended, as students, singly and in pairs, were called into the dean's office. Fortunately, the proctor of the men's dormitory hadn't heard a murmur that evening. There had been no undue noise and hilarity. When I was questioned, I said that I hadn't heard a thing, either. It really was the quietest drunken bout I'd ever known. So the proctor knew nothing. Nobody seemed to know anything. Even George said that the lad who had started the story in the first place had made it up out of his own imagination. Then the empty Angelica wine bottle was found back of the dormitory, where someone had foolishly thrown it. It was placed on the desk of the president for everyone to see.

A special prayer meeting of the faculty was called for that afternoon. We all knelt down by our chairs, and in turn each one of us asked forgiveness for the sinners and the disgraceful scandal that had smirched the honor of Fairmount.

When it came my turn to pray, I remembered what I had advised George about the superior merits of whisky, and so said earnestly and emotionally, "Please forgive them for drinking Angelica wine!"

"Amen, Brother Glick! Amen!" exclaimed the Professor of Biblical Literature.

Later he complimented me saying, "That was a fine, sincere prayer. Simply and to the point you said exactly what troubles all of us. If we could only forgive them for drinking—of all things—Angelica wine."

Since the culprits were among the most prominent students on the campus, the affair was soon hushed up. No one was punished. But in the dean's office there was drawn up a pledge to abstain from "all distilled, fermented, and malt liquors, including wine, beer, and hard cider." The entire student body signed it.

Every precaution was taken that such an incident would never occur again. This extended even to censorship of a play I had in rehearsal at that time. We were doing Shaw's comedy *You Never Can Tell.* The Dean of Women read the play and called me into her office.

"There's drinking in this play," she said, "and we'll have to change it. We cannot afford at this time to lay ourselves open to criticism."

So we rewrote Mr. Shaw, and that made everything perfectly proper. Even the second act, where Dolly, becoming impatient, says, "I'll go and have my cigarette on the beach," we changed to, "I'll go and read my French novel on the beach." And in the last act, where claret cup is freely drunk, we made it, instead, claret lemonade. However, when one character demands hard liquor, we fixed that up nicely by having him say, "Make mine plain soda."

However, the high moral tone we gave to Bernard Shaw was

quite ruined by our next production, Thompson Buchanan's light comedy A Woman's Way. There was one character, a crusty old gentleman, who said "damn" occasionally. That had to come out, of course; and I cautioned all the actors in the play to refrain from ever using that word, both on stage and off.

We rented a theater over in town and reserved the boxes for the president and his wife, the Dean of Women, and other important members of the faculty. I don't know what got into the lad playing the part of the crusty old man. Perhaps it was nervousness, but he forgot my warning and said "damn." Not once but several times. The other actors must have been nervous, too, for they all began to say "damn," even though it wasn't in their lines.

The legitimate laughs we expected from the play didn't come. Most of the audience were too intent on observing the surprised faces of the faculty in the boxes to get the humor of the play. And, since the faculty greeted the performance in gloomy silence, no one had the courage to laugh.

Naturally, I was blamed. The next morning, every member of the faculty took pains to tell me how shocked he had been. I had no apology to offer.

We had planned to present this play in a small near-by town, and to keep the performance from being canceled I practically had to get upon my bended knee and take an oath that everything would be correct and pure. But we went to Belle Plaine and quite redeemed ourselves.

The comment in the college paper on this performance said, "Each member of the cast stalled through all his speeches, carefully stepped over or dodged all swear words. They had been directed to put on an expurgated performance, and so they followed orders to the letter—expurgated it to death. Harry Summers supplied the 'fiddlesticks' where his swear words came, and Paul Well-man said, 'Blooey, blooey!' "

But even this attempt to make the play one hundred percent pure did not help. There were some members of the faculty who accused me of having had a hand in writing that newspaper story. How right they were!

So, despite my well-meant efforts to lead an upright life, I was viewed with suspicion. Someone had even reported to the president that I had been seen smoking a "coffin nail" in broad daylight on the streets of Wichita. Then one day I was invited to a dance in town. I went, and had a wonderful time. The dean invited me into his office and asked for an explanation.

I said, without apology, that I was a member of the Episcopal Church and that there was no ban on dancing among the Episcopalians. In fact, I pointed out that the church encouraged dancing, as it was considered a healthful, normal outlet for the emotions of young people. I could have added, but didn't, that I felt that dancing was better than unchaperoned walks in the moonlight among the cornfields, where the conversation, if I was any judge of human nature, was not all devoted to the discussion of botany and tomorrow's lessons.

I was very much in the dog house.

One morning in February I had just finished a class when I was told that the advance man of the John E. Kellard Company wished to see me. I was delighted, because Kellard was a well-known Shakespearean actor of the day, who trouped from town to town playing *Hamlet*. His advance man wanted to arrange to place tickets at a cut rate for the Fairmount students. I was glad to do what I could.

I walked him to the car line. As he boarded the streetcar he said, "Be at the hotel tonight at six o'clock and have dinner with me."

The way he said it wasn't an invitation. It was a command. And it irritated me.

"Sorry," I replied, "but I've another engagement."

"No, you haven't," he answered, smiling. He spoke the truth. "You'll be there!"

Then he handed me a folder about himself and waved good-by. The folder intrigued me. It read, SAGERSON—THE SEER OF THE STAGE, and contained comments made about him by most of the famous actors and actresses of the day, such as Viola Allen, Alice Fischer, Sir Henry Irving, Theda Bara, and others, as well as such well-known persons as Alexander Graham Bell, Ella Wheeler Wilcox, Lillian Nordica, and David Bispham.

My curiosity concerning Sagerson was aroused. Here, I felt, would be a man worth knowing, and perhaps he might help and advise me about my plays. I was at the hotel promptly at six. Sagerson was a vibrant personality. It was difficult to tell his age, for although his hair was streaked with white, he had a young face and friendly Irish eyes. Now, I had often been to fortunetellers, and had even, now and then, attended services at the spiritualist church.

But at dinner that evening, without going into a trance or calling upon a spirit guide, he began to tell me more things about myself and make more prophecies for the future than all the mediums I had known rolled into one. He also told me about himself.

He had been born in Johnstown, Pennsylvania, and, being stage-struck, came to New York in 1900. Nobody seemed willing to engage him as an actor, but he did find employment as a company manager for theatrical troupes and also as a publicity man. He was happy in this line of endeavor, for he was part of the theater world.

"Everybody else was happier, too," he said, "for I would have been just another bad actor."

Then he discovered he had an unusual gift. Often, seeing people for the first time, he'd suddenly get what he called a "hunch" about them.

One day, strolling along Broadway, he saw a woman standing in front of a store, seemingly unheeding the crowds that were passing by. Something urged him to speak to her and tell her the thought that flashed through his mind.

Abruptly he said, "Don't do what you are planning!"

She stared at him in amazement. "Impertinence," she exclaimed, angrily. "How dare you!"

Embarrassed, Sagerson moved on. But the woman turned and followed him.

"Why did you do that?" she asked, almost apologetically.

Sagerson didn't exactly know. He had felt that, somehow or other, she was headed for trouble, and something had warned him of this. That was why he had spoken so impulsively.

The woman, whose name Sagerson never learned, began to cry.

"Perhaps you are right," she said. "I have quarreled with my husband and am leaving him for another man. But how did you, a stranger to me, know this?"

"I didn't, exactly. It was just a hunch," replied Sagerson. "Maybe it was mental telepathy. I don't know. I merely had the feeling that what you are planning to do is wrong. Forgive me if I have spoken out of turn. But do please think it over carefully."

He gave her his name and address and went his way, leaving her staring after him.

Some time later she wrote him a letter, reminding him of the in-

cident and saying, "I took your advice. God bless you." The letter
was signed, "The woman whose soul you saved."

At first this getting hunches about people rather frightened Sagerson. He was a devout Catholic, and this sort of thing smacked somewhat of fortunetelling. He discussed the matter with his mother.
She felt that he had been unusually blessed with this psychic gift
for helping people. If in this vale of tears a word of cheer and encouragement might bring comfort to many a distressed soul, why
not? But she made him promise never to commercialize his gift and
always to use this power for good.

One night he went to see a performance by a stock company of
Oliver Twist, at the old Murray Hill Theater in New York. In the
cast was a young actress playing a minor part. Having one of his
hunches, he hastily wrote her a post card, saying, "To Frances Starr,
who will someday be a Broadway star."

Frances Starr framed this card and always had it with her in her
dressing room, even in the days when she was one of Belasco's most
famous actresses.

Stories like this about Sagerson are legion. And many a now-
famous player has said that meeting Sagerson and having him tell
them his hunch was the beginning of their success. His prophecies
came true, and his fame in the theater world spread. Prominent
producers, playwrights, and players came to him for tips. When he
had a hunch, he told it. When he didn't, he remained silent.

But he could never get a hunch about himself or his own affairs.

"When I have the choice between managing two plays," he said
smilingly, "I invariably pick the wrong one—the play that fails. I
can tell other people what they should do to reap success—but for
myself, I simply don't know the answer. And when I'm broke—as

I often have been—I don't know what to do. Perhaps my only wealth is my gift and the opportunity I have to help other people."

I asked him if he had an explanation of this gift for character reading and his hunches.

"I don't think I have an unusual gift at all," he answered. "I believe almost anyone can do what I can—providing they have in their hearts great tenderness and sympathy for other people. Everyone consciously or unconsciously gives out a bit of their real personality, no matter how they may try to disguise their own true natures. It's an old bromide, but many a kindly soul covers up his sensitivity with a gruff exterior. See behind that exterior and you see the real person.

"Any man can foretell his own future if he wants to make the supreme effort. But if a man dedicates his life to helping others, he needn't worry about his own future. That will take care of itself, joyfully and happily. Each man has his own personality. He brings it into the world and he takes it out again. Is there any sense in living your life like Eliza crossing the ice? Why hop about from one cake of doubt and fear to another? Why rush to find someone like myself to ask if you are going to marry, and what his or her name is? Such things are merely silly. It isn't necessary to go to mediums and fortunetellers. If there is an unseen world about us, we can discover it for ourselves. You have the answer to all your problems in your own heart, if you will but examine it carefully. It's as simple as that!"

But that evening I talked with him in Wichita, I was not yet able to look into my own heart and find the answer—and I still haven't succeeded. Consequently, I wondered what he would predict for me and what "hunches" he had—if any.

He laughed as he replied, "It's obvious. You want to be a playwright. That you've already told me. Someday you will have a play on Broadway—but I don't see it making you happy. But mark this down—your career as a playwright will start in just about a year from now. And another thing—it won't be at Fairmount College, for I don't see you in this environment much longer."

As I bade him good night, he said, "Keep in touch with me. I'll be seeing you in New York one of these days!"

This was in February of 1917, and one prophecy he made came true faster than I had anticipated.

❧❧

9

COFFEE IN BED

ON THAT morning in April of 1917 when the newspaper boys were shouting in the streets, "Extra! Extra! Extra! United States Declares War on Germany!" I was sound asleep in bed. I had been up late the night before, busy with rehearsals of a play. So I slept until noon. There was no thought in my mind of ever going to war. Wars were fought by professional soldiers—which was one thing, certainly, that I was not.

Then came the announcement of the draft, and I knew that, one of these days, I'd have to go. But the idea didn't fill me with enthusiasm. I was at that time just beginning to sell short sketches and stories to the magazines, and some of my one-act plays had also been accepted for magazine publication. It wasn't easy to give all that up and face an unpredictable and unknown future. So, like everyone else, I fussed and fumed, stormed a bit, and made my will. I didn't see myself as a hero. In fact, I was quite certain that if anybody started shooting at me, I'd run like hell. And the very thought of having to be out of bed at the crack of dawn and doing setting-up exercises made me slightly sick at my stomach. What a hell of a soldier I'd make!

The army felt the same way about me. After a careful physical examination I was found to have not only flat feet but asthma, jumpy nerves, a stigmatism in one eye, and a number of other minor defects that I won't go into. So the army classified me A-2 (as it was called in those days), which meant, "Not fit for combat duty."

So, at first I was assigned to a labor battalion. This meant that I was kept busy cleaning the drilling fields of rocks and debris, assisting in building stone walls, and cleaning up the barracks and the latrines. I was getting $18 a month, with board and room, but I couldn't quite see myself ever getting rich. It looked as if I'd be a private all during the war.

However, my first promotion came rather quickly. One morning when standing inspection the captain growled as he saw the way I had made my bed.

"Don't you know better?" he stormed.

"No, sir!"

"Why not?" he snapped.

The only way out was to tell him the truth. "At home I always had my bed made for me, sir," I replied. "Perhaps the captain can show me the proper way to make a bed."

He growled a bit but, being a good sport, made the bed properly. Then he tore it apart and said, "Now let's see you do it."

I did, three times in a row. He should have been satisfied with my efforts, but he wasn't. That evening, as we stood retreat, I received my first promotion. I was made K.P., with orders to report to the kitchen at four o'clock the next morning.

The cook in charge was a fat, jovial Italian from Kansas City. Now, all good soldiers always gripe about the food. But I belong to the school of thought that holds that honey catches more flies than vinegar. So I promptly told the cook his food was the best I'd ever eaten. This pleased him. It was his first wartime compliment. And since I had a lean and hungry look, he decided he'd fatten me up

a bit. So, late at night when the last pot was scrubbed and the
garbage disposed of, he'd give me a sly wink. Then from the icebox
he'd produce two large, fat, juicy steaks and a bottle of red wine
he had smuggled into camp. I was K.P. for a whole week, and thoroughly enjoyed it. I would just as soon have remained in the kitchen,
but the captain decided to vary the routine.

My next assignment was guard duty. None of us guards was to
be trusted with a gun, it seems; so armed with sticks we'd march up
and down outside the barracks and report at intervals that all was
well. Guard duty, too, I found very pleasant. It was something of
a relief, being alone at night under the starry sky and watching the
dawn come creeping up over the hills.

Now, I was becoming quite resigned to the thought that my
career as a soldier would be spent in this prosaic manner. I had
hoped that I might be assigned to something a trifle more exciting,
even if I wasn't fit for combat. And then one day it happened. I was
summoned to the captain's office.

He looked me over sternly as he said, "I have an order here
transferring you to the Intelligence Office at Camp Headquarters.
How come?"

I scratched my head and looked puzzled as I answered, "I guess
it's because I've had a college education, sir."

"Think you can handle this?" he asked.

I rose nobly to the occasion. "I've done my best as K.P. and on
guard duty, sir," I responded. "I can only try to do my best in whatever situation I am unfortunately placed."

He didn't seem to be too impressed, as he replied, "Of all places
to send *you*—the Intelligence Office."

"Yes, sir!" I answered.

"If you run into any spies, don't shoot before you see the whites of their eyes."

"Yes, sir!—No, sir, I mean," I said.

Spies—so that's what I'd be coming in contact with! I could hardly wait for him to sign the transfer and march off with my barracks bag over my shoulders. Spies! What an opportunity to get material for stories! At that moment I loved the army and was happy to be a soldier.

But it didn't take me long to learn that I had been sent to the Intelligence Office because I had had theatrical experience, and was also a writer. My duty, as such, was to ramble around the camp, find out what entertainments were being given, and what else was being done to keep the soldiers happy, and then write reports on the various activities.

There weren't many of us in the office: a few enlisted men, a lieutenant, and a commanding officer, Major Eugene E. Barton. Major Barton was a regular army man and had served with General Pershing in the Philippines. He commanded our entire respect and loyalty. Sometimes I think he groaned inwardly at us "civilian soldiers" with flat feet, but he was patient with us, and he knew we were not exactly popular with the lads in the other offices at headquarters. We acquired the reputation of being busybodies—totally deserved. Now and then some of the soldiers in other offices would send us memos, addressed to the Commissary Department of the Quartermasters, saying, "Please furnish immediately Private X of the Intelligence Office with one pair of gumshoes and one lip switch."

But we never went around in disguise. All we did was try to be as friendly as we could with everybody and endeavor to find out all we could about them, where they came from, who their friends were, and how they liked army life.

There was one chap, a top sergeant in the printing office where our orders were all mimeographed, who particularly didn't like me. He was from the deep South, and since I was from Iowa I was a "Damnyank, and it's one word, too!"

One morning an order which I had written and which the major had signed was slow in coming back. We were in a hurry. So I rushed over to the printing office to see what was causing the unnecessary delay.

When I asked the top sergeant, he replied sweetly, "They've been held up because I had to correct your English!"

I hit the ceiling. I had had stories published, and as an author took myself very seriously. "You damn Yank!" I said. "Correct my English? *My English?* You can't even read!"

He hit the ceiling. He outranked me, and in the presence of the entire office force called me to attention. I snapped into it. Then he laid me out—good and low. He fought once again, to his entire satisfaction and the honor of his forefathers, the Battle of Bull Run. I had to stand and take it. When he had finally finished giving me total and complete hell, he dismissed me. I crawled back to my office.

I told the major what had happened. He didn't make a comment, just buttoned up his coat, rose, and walked into the printing office. He called the entire staff to attention and told them in good old army language that whenever an order came from his office signed with his name, not a word, not a comma, not even a period was to be changed. The top sergeant turned red in the face.

When he got back to our office, he called me to his desk and told me what he had done. Then he murmured softly, so that no one else could hear him, "Tell me, was the English in that order perfectly correct?"

From that time on, had he asked me to stand on my head in a watering trough designed for horses, I would have done so gladly and without a murmur. And just to prove he liked my reports, the major promoted me to sergeant. That put me in the same social class with the top sergeant in the printing office, and in time we got so that we even spoke to each other.

I have always been grateful to the major for his advice about interviewing people. "We're just a bunch of old snoops in this office," he said. "But I've found that people will tell you anything if you go at it right. Play dumb, smile, appear casual, not too eager, be almost indifferent, and when you ask an innocent question, people will think you're just another dumb bastard and will tell you what you want to know. Be polite and friendly—that's the answer."

Since that time, in my career as a busybody in getting material for stories, I've found that when I apply this principle, it usually works.

One afternoon I was quietly reading a magazine—there being nothing else to do at the moment. The major, observing me perfectly relaxed, said ironically, "Sergeant, you're overworked. You need an assistant!"

"Yes, sir," I responded quickly and went into action. I typed out the usual form and handed it to the major. He had to sign it.

Shortly afterwards a pale-faced corporal appeared at the office and said, hesitantly, "I've been told to report to Sergeant Glick."

Hoping to put him at his ease, for he was very nervous, I said jovially, "I've been expecting you. Sit down, and tell me what you've been up to lately."

He turned even paler as he stammered, "Well—you see—I—"

I sensed that I had said the wrong thing, for he was one of the most frightened men I'd met in a long time.

"Let's go to the canteen and have a coke," I suggested.

I led the way. When I handed him the bottle with a straw in it, his hands trembled.

"Why do you buy me a coke?" he managed to murmur.

"Thought you might be thirsty," I said. "What's your first name?"

"Fred—and it's my real name, too," he replied.

"You type, Fred?" I asked. He nodded. "Can you take shorthand, too, Fred?" He nodded again.

"Well, how would you like to be assigned to duty in the Intelligence Office?"

He laid down the bottle. "I don't get it—I don't get it," he muttered weakly. "Where can we go where I can talk without being overheard?"

Not far from headquarters was a road leading into the woods beyond the camp. We took our bottles and headed that way. Finding a quiet spot, we sat down by the side of the road. Then he managed to tell me his story.

He was married. His wife was living in Little Rock, but he hadn't seen her in two long months. He had been in Officer's Candidate School, but hadn't quite made the grade and had been dropped. He was very bitter about it, and what he had said at that time about the army wasn't fit to be repeated in the best military circles.

"I shouldn't have said those things," he went on. "I should have known I'd be reported. And when I got an order to appear at the Intelligence Office, I knew it was the end for me. I expected to be court-martialed and shot. I thought I had disgraced my family and shamed my wife. Instead, you ask me how would I like to work there. Me? After all the things I've said? I don't get it—I don't get it!"

I quickly explained.

"You mean I'm not going to be court-martialed and shot?"

"No! I've said things, too. Forget it."

"And I can see my wife once again?"

"Certainly. We'll go back to the office, fix you up a pass for town —and you needn't report back until noon tomorrow."

It was at that moment that he broke down and cried. So did I.

He came back promptly at noon the next day, smiling and happy, but even paler than he had been the day before. It was easily arranged for him to have a pass for town every night, and when the day's work was done, he'd catch a bus and off he'd go.

One evening as we were closing our desks, he said, "Will you do something for me?"

"Sure," I replied.

"Let's stand retreat tonight."

Now, since we were at headquarters there was quite a ceremony every evening at retreat, with the band playing *The Star-Spangled Banner*. Those working in the offices were not required to be present, for often our duties kept us busy at that hour.

But that evening Fred and I stood at attention during retreat, and when the band played the national anthem there were tears in his eyes.

As he jumped aboard the bus for town, he gave me a friendly salute, and said, "Long may she wave, pal!"

"Amen!" I echoed.

And every evening after that, save when our duties prevented it,

Fred and I felt that it was a privilege to stand retreat. We were both proud to be Americans, and we hadn't really meant the uncomplimentary remarks we had made about the army.

But there was one sergeant in our office who got into trouble and really was court-martialed. This was George, the file clerk. He was a silent, moody lad, and the most we ever saw of him around the office was his back, as he stood filing away papers. Evenings now and then, when some of us would seek entertainment at the movies or the canteens, at first we'd always ask George to go along. But he invariably declined. He preferred to sit around the barracks doing nothing. Finally we gave up asking him. He simply wasn't one of the gang, and there was nothing we could do about it. We went our way, and left him alone to amuse himself. We'd hand him papers to be filed. He'd file them, and that was that. Then one day he asked for a pass to town, the first he'd ever wanted. And off he went, on his own. We wondered what he'd do in town—go sit at a table in the public library, staring at a book?

The next morning George didn't return on time. He wasn't back by noon. We were puzzled as to what might have happened to him, or what he had done. But as far as we could discover, no papers were missing from the files. Then, late that afternoon two M.P.'s appeared at the office, bringing with them tousled, bleary-eyed, and drooping George.

The M.P.'s told us the story. George had confessed everything. Getting into town, he got hold of a bottle of corn liquor, and at the same time obtained possession of a gun—a toy pistol from the ten-cent store. Then, fortified by the liquor and armed with the gun, somewhere or other he ran into another soldier in town on a pass. He rammed the gun in this soldier's back and headed him for the nearest alley. There, waving the toy pistol, George made the soldier do "Squads right," "Squads left," salute, and stand at attention. When the M.P.'s found him, the frightened private was kneeling, asking George not to shoot him!

The major was puzzled. Should George be sent away to have his sanity examined—or what? Then George broke down and poured out his heart to the major. He said he couldn't stand it any longer. Here were the rest of us in the office, running around camp and having something of an exciting time, and all he did was file our blasted reports. He was damned sick and tired of it all. He said he wasn't the least bit sorry for what he had done, either, and that he had enjoyed ordering someone else around for a change.

The major frowned, then said, "I'm going to have you court-martialed and sent to the stockade."

And that's exactly what happened to George. We'd stop around now and then, taking him cigarettes and candy. But George was a changed boy. He was smiling and happy, even though he was behind barbed wires. He didn't seem to mind being in prison in the least. In fact, he seemed actually to be enjoying himself. It was a strange case.

Then one day, rambling about camp I ran into George.

"Escaped?" I asked.

"Hell, no," he answered. "I'm a trusty!"

From a hint the major dropped I suspected something along this line, but I wanted to hear George's version. We sought a secluded spot where we couldn't be overheard, and George told me the truth.

He said, "The major wanted a confidential agent in the stockade —and I'm it. I'm like some of the rest of you fellows now—but it's a damned sight more dangerous—as I'm living among real criminals. I make my reports to the major—but someone else files them! I'm having the best time, living in the stockade, I've had in this

man's army. Don't you go worrying about me.—If I can manage
to get off tonight, maybe I'll see you at the movies."

From that time on, George was one of the gang. Months later,
when the war was over and I was discharged, George was still in the
army, still living in the stockade, and liking it very much indeed.

Then I got caught doing something for which I should have been
court-martialed, too, I suppose. One of my one-act plays, *The
Fourth Mrs. Phillips,* which I had sold while in civilian life, was
published in a magazine. Pete, who was a sergeant, too, and came
from Oklahoma, had never met a live author before. He bought a
copy of the magazine and asked if I'd autograph it for him. Would
I? This was the first time anyone had asked that of me.

"Thanks," said Pete. "Gosh—I wish I could do something for
you!"

As if he hadn't done enough, by giving my ego a big boost up-
wards! But I had an idea.

"There is something you can do," I said.

Now, Pete belonged to Headquarters Company. I was assigned
to what was called Headquarters Detachment Company. In this
branch were all of us who worked in the offices at headquarters. We
never did K.P., we never stood guard duty, and we didn't even have
to police or clean up the barracks. We merely made our beds in the
morning, and at mealtime walked into the dining room, sat down
at the table, and ate like gentlemen. The K.P. duty, policing, and so
forth was done by the lads in the Headquarters Company, of which
Pete was one.

Breakfast, mornings, was from six to seven. Usually I'd miss it. I
could drop in at the canteen near by and have a cup of coffee and
a hard-boiled egg, or a sandwich, before appearing at the office at

eight o'clock. But I thought it would be a fine idea if Pete would bring me a cup of hot coffee in bed. Then I could snooze a little longer, until time to get up in a leisurely fashion. Pete was delighted to oblige. So he brought me my coffee, and I had coffee in bed while in the army. But not, as it happened, for long. The captain in charge of Headquarters Company somehow got wind of it. I think some jealous so-and-so reported me. I was called into the captain's office.

He said graciously, "I hear, Sergeant, you've been having coffee in bed, mornings."

"Yes, sir," I responded, equally gracious.

"I presume in civilian life you always had coffee in bed," he asked, still being very polite.

"No, sir—never!"

At that he exploded. "Then why—# % $ & ¾ ! ! !—in the army!"

"It's the principle of the thing, sir," I said.

"Blooey," he groaned. "Suppose everybody in the army wanted their coffee in bed mornings—what sort of an old ladies' home would this be? Let me ask you another question. Do you really like having coffee in bed?"

"Not particularly, sir," I replied, and added: "If the captain wishes to order me to put a stop to this bad habit, I'd be only too glad to obey the captain's orders."

"Thank you, Sergeant, for seeing eye to eye with me on this matter!" he muttered bitterly.

Somehow or other, by the underground, the major heard of this. Then one morning he arrived at the office earlier than usual, and nobody was around to say "Good morning, sir" to him. He felt lonely. When we finally trooped in, he merely grinned and said nothing. Later that day an order was posted. It said that we were all to join the other men in Headquarters Detachment Company for setting-up exercises at seven o'clock in the morning.

There was only one way to show our appreciation of this. We got word to a reporter on the camp newspaper and he came around for an interview. And our thanks to the major were well expressed in a newspaper story, which said in part:

> How often has it been said that the office man accustomed to wearing the stiff collar and having dainty hands would never make a good soldier? Times without number. But the men of the headquarters who spend their time slinging ink with pens, pushing the pencil or punching the A.B.C.'s are daily giving the lie to that statement. They have decided to be real soldiers. . . . The men get out every morning for 45 minutes of brisk exercise, known as the morning physical culture class. . . . Sergeant Glick is one of the most enthusiastic members of the morning class. Sergeant Glick detests such early advent into the cool morning air of Camp Pike, but once he gets out of doors performs his work with precision. . . . However, these men are feeling better for their efforts and find the day's work is easier attacked after a brisk workout in the keen morning air.

When the major read this news story he asked me, "Sergeant, did you write this?"

"No, sir," I answered, modestly. "But I helped inspire it!"

"Thank you, Sergeant, thank you," mumbled the major.

Finally the war was over and I was listed for discharge. I had a job waiting for me as director of the Community Theater of Waterloo, Iowa. The war with Germany was over, but for me the battle of the dowagers would now commence again. In a way I was sorry to be discharged. I had no complaint against army life. I had had very little discipline—regrettably, for it would have been good for me. I had had a soft berth in an office, with work that was interesting. The major summed up my war experience one day when the commanding office of the near-by air base dropped into our office. I had never been up in a plane, and said so. I was told that if I would come over to the base I'd get a ride.

"Look, Sergeant," said the major. "You fought the Battle of Camp Pike with a pen—why do you want to risk your life, now that the war is over?"

On the day that I left, after saying good-by, I paused a moment in the door, stood at attention, and gave the major a whole-hearted, sincere salute—as one does to a man you respect. Then I tried to do a proper about-face, tripped, and practically fell upon my nose.

The major's last words to me were, "Sergeant, you're one hell of a soldier!"

I never saw him again, but some years later I had the pleasure of meeting the man who had once been his commanding officer, General Pershing. It was during the American Legion convention at San Antonio, Texas. I was staying at the Hotel Menger, and one noon, walking through the patio, I ran into General Pershing.

"I'm lost," he said. "I'm supposed to have lunch here today with Lord Allenby. Where do I go?"

"I don't know, sir," I answered, truthfully.

"Why don't you?" he snapped, in true soldierly fashion.

"Because I didn't open the general's invitation. Who did?"

He grinned, patted me on the shoulder and said, "I know—I know. Relax. But could you help an old soldier find out where he's supposed to eat?"

I hastily summoned a bellboy, and explained the dilemma.

"Wait a minute," said the bellboy, and vanished.

In a few seconds he came back with five more bellboys. They drew up in soldierly fashion, saluted General Pershing, and then proudly said, "Come with us, sir. This way, sir!"

"Thank you, gentlemen. Thank you," said General Pershing. "This is the way I like to see things done."

And escorted by six happy and grinning Negro bellboys, off he marched. For me, at that moment, World War I was officially over

10

THE BATTLE OF THE DOWAGERS

WATERLOO, IOWA, has two of everything. A river runs through the center of town, marking the boundary line between the East Side and the West Side. Consequently, there are two public libraries, two churches of every denomination, two high schools, and so on. But when I went to Waterloo, there was only one Community Theater, and that, I believe, was quite sufficient for the drama-loving citizens, united in a common bond.

It was the first community theater I had ever directed. In the beginning I hadn't the slightest knowledge of what to do or how to go about it. But I was soon to learn.

Every morning after the opening night of a play, I always remained in bed until noon. Not that I was too tired out, but because the telephone by my bedside rang constantly. Those phoning would be the dowagers, our best friends and our severest critics.

The first to phone would usually be Madge X. She bounced out of bed early to get breakfast for her three handsome children and her dyspeptic husband. Once the children were safely off to school, and her husband on his way to his office, Madge had the rest of the day to devote to her cultural activities. Madge believed heart and soul in the uplift of the drama, and she also liked to act. Just why, I could never determine. But certainly she didn't believe in hiding her talent beneath a bushel. And it would have taken a huge bushel basket to conceal the rotund Madge.

"I saw your play last night," she'd say, and without pausing for breath would add ominously, "I didn't like it! I hope you don't mind honest criticism?"

"Not at all," I'd murmur. "I welcome it. That's how we can all learn, improve our plays, and raise the standards."

Now, what our standards really were, I was never able to determine. But we always strove to raise them, just the same.

Then Madge would say, "It isn't any criticism of your work as director. Under the circumstances you did all that was humanly possible. "But why—why—did you cast Agnes in the leading role?"

"She's a patron member, like you," I'd answer truthfully. "She's subscribed fifty dollars—so why shouldn't she be entitled to a leading role now and then?"

"But whoever told *her* she could act? I thought she was awful. And my husband thought so, too."

(I once called Madge's bluff on that one. Meeting her husband on the street one day, I said to him, "I understand you didn't like the play last night." "Who said so?" he asked dourly. "Your wife." "I didn't say I liked it or didn't like it. How do I know? I slept through the whole damn thing.")

Then to clinch her argument, Madge would add, "Blanche didn't like the play, either. She walked out after the second act."

"She always does that," I'd reply. "She left after the second act of the play you were in, too."

"Yes—I know. But that evening her daughter was ill. What are you going to give next?"

I'd mention the name of the light drawing-room comedy we had in mind. Drawing-room comedies were very popular with our public, provided they contained a leading role in which a dowager could appear, wear a few new gowns, rattle some teacups effectively, and have playing opposite her some handsome young man about town.

"Is the play cast yet?" Madge would ask.

"Not yet," I'd say, and knowing what was on her mind, I would hint delicately, "What about you playing the leading role?"

"I'm much too busy. Then, too, I'm certain my husband wouldn't like it. He wants me home evenings.—However, I'd like to read the play. Why don't you come and have tea with me this afternoon, and bring a copy?"

"Thank you," I'd murmur. And I knew the die was cast, even though I'd have to do a lot of coaxing and she'd decline the role as many times as Caesar cast aside the crown. But when I'd tell her that if she didn't want to do the part I'd probably have to ask Blanche, Madge would say, "What—her? Let me read the play again. I'll ask my husband and see what he thinks."

He invariably "thought so, too"—and so Madge was the leading lady in the next play, and that made everybody unhappy save herself.

After Madge's phone call, Blanche would ring me.

"I saw your play last night," she'd say sweetly.

"All of it?" I'd ask, just as sweetly.

"Only the first two acts. That was enough for me. Why did you cast Agnes in the leading role, and whoever told her she could act? Of course, this is quite confidential, and Agnes is one of my dearest friends, but she simply can't act—and my husband thinks so, too.—What are you going to give next?"

I'd mention the title of the light drawing-room comedy.

"I've read it," Blanche would say. "There's a good leading role in that play."

"I wish I could persuade you to do it," I'd murmur, keeping my fingers crossed.

"I can't. I've already had one part this year, and if I played another, everyone would hate me. You'd be criticized, too."

"I guess you're right," I'd reply, and unwind my fingers.

"But I've been reading a very good comedy that perhaps you might want to do next year. Come over and have tea with me soon, and let's talk it over.—Good-by for now—and don't you tell Agnes I didn't stay to the bitter, bitter end last night."

By noon Agnes herself would ring. "I've been trying to get you all morning," she'd say. "But your line has been busy."

"Yes," I'd answer. "Everyone has been phoning, saying how perfectly wonderful you were last night. It was a triumph!"

"I've heard so, too," Agnes would say. "My friends have been ringing me all morning. Blanche phoned, saying she was sorry she couldn't stay for the last act, but her daughter has been ill and she had to go home. However, she's coming again tonight, as she says she wouldn't miss it for worlds."

"Nobody would. When you appear in a play, the whole town turns out—and they've all been talking about you this morning."

"That's what Madge said, too. She said I looked perfectly stunning last night, and it was wonderful how I remembered that long part and didn't miss a line.—I wonder what the paper will say tonight."

"There'll be a good review—don't worry," I'd assure her.

And it was good. I knew it would be—since I had written the review myself. For quite a time in Waterloo I always wrote the reviews

of the plays I directed. The task of reviewing my own plays wasn't
something I had sought with malice aforethought. It was wished on
me. At one of our early efforts an impertinent young squirt from
the newspaper was sent to cover the play. He not only covered it—
he buried it! He didn't like the play. He didn't like the costumes.
He didn't like the acting, and especially he didn't like Mamie
M——'s interpretation of the leading role, and said so. He was too
truthful in his review, and that was what hurt.

The next day the managing editor of the paper asked me to
lunch.

"I'm in a hell of a jam," he said. "Mamie is sore about what the
paper has said. She's been raising hell all day, phoning the paper,
having all her friends phone, and even her husband has phoned
raising a squawk. He's one of our best advertisers, too.—Now don't
misunderstand me. I think the community theater is a fine cultural
activity, and worthy of support—and the policy of our paper is to
support and encourage every deserving movement in town. But migawd—why does Mamie think she can act? I've known her all my
life, and what's got into her? And just because an honest reporter
told the truth—see what's happened?"

"What has?" I asked.

"Her husband threatens to withdraw his advertising. That's what.
So what are we to do?"

"Give us good reviews," I suggested.

"What's a good review?"

"Praise everybody—especially the leading ladies," I said. "Roast
me if you like. I get paid for directing the plays. But the gals who act
give their time and talent—and do it for love." Then, remembering
what Gussie had once said to me, I added, "What's business to me
is pleasure for them."

"If we praise them—we'll only encourage them," he said bitterly.

"But that's the purpose of our community theater: to encourage and develop artistic endeavors and bring to light the hidden creative spirit of the townspeople. In time—who knows?—Waterloo may become the art center of the world."

He gave me a dour look. "I still don't know what a good review is," he muttered.

"Let me write the next review—and then you can keep it on file in the newspaper as a model."

"Okay," he answered.

After that, the day before the opening performance I always wrote the review of the play, and it was safe at the newspaper office even before the curtain rose on the first act. And they were good reviews, too, no matter what the dowagers in the audience might think or say about the efforts of their rivals. But everybody was happy. Our membership increased, and the newspaper had no more trouble with their advertisers.

I presume that I might have continued to write all the reviews during my stay in Waterloo but for an unforeseen occurrence—one of those things defined as "an act of God." As usual, before the first performance of one of our plays, my review was safely in the hands of the editor. I was at the theater early that evening to see that the actors were all on hand, the properties in place, and the stage set as it should be. There was a hurried call from the women's dressing room. Sophie, who was taking one of the minor roles, had suddenly become ill. There was turmoil. A doctor was hastily summoned. Sophie had acute appendicitis, and was hurried to the hospital.

But the play must go on. We rushed the prompter into the part. She halfway knew all the lines, anyway. So that evening she played the role and played it well. But I had forgotten about the review, in which I had made special mention of Sophie, and had been specific about her acting in certain scenes. The next day the review appeared as usual. No mention was made of the substitution, and not a word of praise for the understudy.

"Who wrote that review?" an irate patron of the arts phoned the paper the next morning. "Didn't he know that Sophie was taken to the hospital for an operation?"

The managing editor did some quick thinking. "We sent a new reporter," he apologized. "Probably got the name from the program. But it won't happen again!"

It didn't, either. I was fired as my own critic. After that, a reporter from the paper always covered the plays. He had been instructed to tread gently, and he did. But when I met him on the street and thanked him for his fine review, he'd always hold his nose in an expressive gesture, and murmur something about selling his soul to keep his job.

Still, no matter how glowing the reviews might be, the next morning after a play the dowagers would always phone me to give their "honest" opinion. It helped me keep a balance and prevented me from becoming too conceited.

Since ours was the first community theater in Iowa, we were truly pioneering in a virgin field. At times we didn't quite know exactly what it was all about. But we did get our plays on the stage, and we had our own theater, too!

At first we gave our plays in rented auditoriums. But it was most unsatisfactory, being orphans and homeless. How could the art of the theater come into its full flowering when we were being chased from pillar to post? So it was decided that we must have a place of our own, a roof over our heads, and a theater to which we alone had the key. The leading ladies and their best friends spent days trudging in and out of alleys, carefully examining old barns, deserted factories, and all types of empty buildings. Finally someone called their attention to an abandoned Methodist church, which the congregation had outgrown. It was ideal, for it already boasted a raised platform at one end that could easily be converted into a stage.

The theater seated 150. It was heated by a hot-air furnace, with the grate down front by the stage. Consequently, those who sat in the first few rows roasted and complained of the heat, while those in the back froze and howled about the cold. But it was Art with a capital A—and our publicity stated that anyone in town who paid five dollars for a season ticket was now part owner of a little theater.

While I was always grateful to the dowagers for their support and encouragement in those early days of trial and error, still everything was very social-social. Good fun, naturally, and I had many a well-balanced dinner and learned to handle a teacup as well as any well-bred member of the local Four Hundred. Yet it irritated me, too. My ideal was that the community theater should belong to the people. Just who the "people" were I wasn't quite certain, but they were certainly around, even though they were floating unattached somewhere in space. I was even fond of paraphrasing the immortal words of Abraham Lincoln, and saying, "Our theater is a theater of the people, by the people, and for the people."

In my opening talk at the first meeting upon my arrival, I strongly stressed this point. I received some applause from the democratically minded citizens present. But one ample-bosomed patron of the arts took me to task afterwards.

She said, oratorically, "Of course I believe in everyone having an equal opportunity in our theater. Certainly we should respect talent, no matter where it may be found. However, if you keep on insisting that this is a theater for the people, there will be a lot of social climbers who will try to get in and run things."

They did, too. But what could be done about it? We had to have an audience, and I felt that anyone who bought a season ticket was entitled to attend our plays and take part in them, too. It didn't matter a bit whether or not they had a birth certificate or were socially housebroken.

In one of our plays there was a young lad who lived four miles out of town. He dearly loved the theater, and even though he had a minor role and walked to town and back, he never missed a rehearsal and was on time, rain or shine. Often the dowagers wouldn't appear because they had a social engagement. This gave me food for thought.

But when, with the zeal of a young but misguided crusader, I began to scout for talent in the highways and byways, there was a lifting of eyebrows. The workers in a factory had a dramatic club of their own. Attending one of their performances, I saw a young girl who, I felt, had unusual ability. She was, as it happened, a maid in one of the better homes. But I gave her a part in a play. Her employer failed to see me when she passed me on the street. But the girl gave an excellent performance. Her morale soared. She took her savings, enrolled in a business school, and ultimately became a very competent secretary. Things like that were warming to the heart, even though it was whispered that certain dowagers hesitated to invite me to tea, lest I make advances to their maids.

We even wrote and produced original plays. I had a class in playwriting, where I told the members all about copyright and other such vital matters. One day a matron who had written a neat little number phoned me in great glee.

"You may now congratulate me!" she exclaimed. "My first play is a success. It has been accepted for copyright in Washington by the Library of Congress!"

Some of the ladies also wrote poetry. There was one who had a whole volume of verse published at her own expense. She lived in a beautiful home across from the park. Looking out of her windows, she was inspired one winter by the barren trees covered with snow and sleet. She therefore called her book *Naked Limbs*. When the book was published, there was a big display in one of the downtown stores, and an enormous poster proclaimed, "Mrs. Blank's *Naked Limbs* For Sale Here."

The ladies, being literary, now and then gave tea parties for visiting authors. I was invited to one given in honor of a former newspaper reporter on one of the local papers. Since leaving Waterloo he had had four novels published, none of which had been too successful. But now he was back in town again, gathering materials (so I was told) for a new novel. Later I read his new novel. Very good it was, too—a book entitled *Main Street*, and the author was Sinclair Lewis.

In the book, as I remember, Carol, the heroine, exhausted herself emotionally in organizing a little theater. I wasn't in Waterloo at the time the book was published, but a friend there wrote me that one of the dowagers had said, "Of course—some little theaters may have been like that. But ours certainly wasn't!"

She had probably forgotten the heartbreaking rehearsals I had had when she played a leading role. I had a terrible time directing in a passionate love scene the handsome young man who was cast as her lover in the play.

"Grab her in your arms," I said. "Look her in the eyes—hold her tight—and kiss her as if you meant it!"

"Yes," said the dowager. "Don't be afraid. We must make this realistic. Kiss me square on the mouth—don't peck me on the cheek. Kiss me! Kiss me!"

After the rehearsal he took me aside.

"Look," he said, a gleam of anger in his eyes. "She's practically old enough to be my mother! I'm engaged to be married. What will my girl think if I kiss her realistically?"

"This is art—not life!" I replied.

"But do I have to go into a clinch at every rehearsal?" he asked.

I could only offer a compromise by saying, "Save your strength for the opening night—and then give her the works."

"Damned if I'll make an ass of myself," he muttered savagely.

He was still shy on the night of the performance. Came the moment of the passionate embrace. He sort of clutched the lady as if she were a sack of dynamite—which she was. She grabbed him, threw her arms around his neck, and gave him a smack loud enough to be heard in the third row. He jumped back, so startled that he practically fell into the footlights.

The next morning, when all the leading lady's dearest friends phoned me, they were unanimous in saying that they thought the love scene was atrociously played, and why hadn't I directed it properly?

But I was not too discouraged. There were some loyal friends who patted me on the back now and then, gave me a word of cheer and encouragement, and understood some of the problems we all had to face. At the time, I thought our headaches and our triumphs, our successes and failures, were unique. But in the years to come, when directing other community theaters in Sarasota, Florida; Columbia,

South Carolina; San Antonio, Texas, and elsewhere, I had the same trials and tribulations, the same joys and help from friends.

All this time, in my spare moments I was writing and writing and writing. And in the meantime another of Sagerson's prophecies had come true. Among the original plays we had produced in Waterloo were several of my own writing. One was accepted for publication by the Walter H. Baker Company of Boston, and I received my complimentary copies in the mails exactly one year and two weeks after my first meeting with Sagerson, as he said I would. Then, too, a few short stories of my writing had been accepted. I had even sold some short sketches to *Smart Set* and had a letter from H. L. Mencken asking for more. I had also written a couple of full-length plays.

I was getting restless and again had itching feet. I didn't know what to do. I wrote to Sagerson and asked his advice. He replied by saying, "Go to New York and try your luck on Broadway. But stop over in Johnstown between trains. I've got a hunch for you."

11

AT HOME ON BROADWAY

WHEN I saw Sagerson in Johnstown, he said, "My hunch is that the one person you should know on Broadway is Alice Fischer. She's a live, vital person, with a generous heart and soul, and one of the most beautiful women in the theater. Just phone her someday when you get to New York and tell her you're a friend of mine."

Back in the 1890's Alice Fischer was a popular star on Broadway. And even though in her later years (at the time I knew her) she didn't always have the leading roles in plays, still she always got a rousing hand of applause from her many friends and admirers on her first entrance. She was still beautiful at fifty, majestic and authoritative, with a kindly sense of humor and a rare genius for helping other people. She gave me good, sound advice, bossed me around, and opened many doors for me. She introduced me to her friends, the famous actors and actresses whom I had seen in the theater and admired from a distance.

We soon became fast friends, and one day she phoned me in great distress. "Are you busy this afternoon," she asked, in a feeble, faraway voice—which was quite unlike Alice, for usually when she spoke she could be heard to the last row in the top balcony.

When I assured her that I had no engagement, she said, "Then come, please, and see me—for the last time. I'm dying!" Abruptly she hung up the receiver.

Frightened and terribly disturbed, I hurried to her apartment.

When I arrived, there were several other good friends of hers assembled in the living room, sad and unhappy. Alice, clad in one of her best gowns, was lying on the settee, a rug thrown over her feet. When I came into the room amid a hushed silence, she feebly raised her hand.

"Who is it now?" she asked, faintly.

"It's me—Carl," I said, choking back the tears.

"Thank you, Carl—for coming. Do please sit down. I'm not well. I'm dying."

"The doctor—" I started to say.

"No need to call him. What can he tell me that I don't know myself? So good of all of you to come," she gasped, and closed her eyes.

"Get a glass of water," someone suggested.

"No water—nothing," murmured Alice. "Just let me be quiet. I want to be surrounded by my good friends when the end comes."

"But Alice," said Ed Borelle, "you'll be with us many, many years yet."

"No—no," protested Alice weakly. "I've had a wonderful life—known a great many people whom I have loved."

"And who love you," said Grace Furniss, tearfully. And we all echoed her sentiments.

"I remember when I first came to New York," Alice went on. "I was only sixteen."

"Don't talk, if it distresses you," I urged.

"No— I want to talk. It helps me—at this moment.—I remember when I left Terre Haute, I was shy, timid, and frightened.

I was facing the world alone. That night, on the train, before getting into my berth, I knelt in the aisles and said my prayers as usual. The porter must have thought it strange, for he asked me if I was ill. 'No,' I said, 'I'm saying my prayers by my bed, just as I always do at home. And I'm asking that God help make me a good actress and a good woman.' And I've been both—although there have been times I've had some terrible parts to play.—But now this is the end, and I hope God will forgive me."

We wiped the tears from our eyes as we assured her that she had been both a good actress and a good woman. In fact, Alice was one of the few actresses I have ever known who didn't drink, smoke, or frequent night clubs. She went to church regularly, and would now and then scold her friends when they told an off-color story.

"When I am gone, I want each one of you to have something to remember me by," she said, gesturing to her treasures. "That clock —Edward VII gave it to Madame Nordica, the opera singer—and Nordica gave it to me."

She told each one of us what she'd like us to have, the day after her funeral. We all protested.

But Alice waved aside our murmurs. "However, I don't know what to do with Will's tights."

William Harcourt was her husband, who had passed away some years previously. He had been a popular leading man, and the tights she referred to were those he had worn when he played Romeo to the Juliet of Maude Adams. Someone suggested that the tights properly belonged in some museum.

"Yes, of course—in a museum. Poor, dear Will—he was such a handsome man," she said sadly, her voice growing fainter and trail-ing off into silence.

We wiped the tears from our eyes. Just then the telephone rang.

"Who is it?" asked Alice, her eyes closed. "Tell them to come over right away—I'm dying."

I answered the phone. "It's George M. Cohan," I said. "He's at the Savoy-Plaza. He says he has a new play he is thinking of producing, and—" this was hard for me to tell her, under the circumstances—"and he thinks there's a part in the play for you."

"A part for me?" asked Alice, in a faint voice.

"Yes. What—what shall I tell him?"

"Tell him nothing. I'll answer the phone!"

We all protested, but Alice threw aside the rug, jumped to her feet, and dashed to the phone.

"Hello, George," she cried, in her natural big, booming voice. "What's this? You're casting a new play and think there's a part in it for me? Certainly I'll come to see you. Yes—yes—right away. I'll get a taxi and be there in no time at all."

She turned to us, beaming. "Wonderful—a part in a new play. Get me a taxi, Ed. How do I look? Where's my hat and coat?"

"But Alice—" we exclaimed.

"But what?" she stormed. "Hurry—get a taxi. I'll not be gone long. Stay here, everybody."

"I'd better go with you," I said.

"Nonsense. I've ridden in taxis for years. I don't need anyone to go along with me."

We couldn't stop her, even if she was dying. And off she went like a whirlwind. Back in the living room we put aside our damp handkerchiefs and looked at each other a trifle sheepishly.

"Alice is just as good an actress off the stage as she is on," someone said.

In an hour Alice was back, sparkling and beaming, and her usual energetic self once again.

"George said I was looking wonderful—never seen me looking better. We had a wonderful time. It's a good part, too—the madame of a bawdy house. What's a bawdy house?" she asked, pretending she didn't know. Someone tactfully explained.

"Well—perhaps I look the type—but certainly I've never been one. Have you, Grace?"

"Alice—how could you?" protested Grace. "But how can you take the part if you're not well?"

"I'm perfectly all right!"

"But an hour ago you said you were dying?" I muttered.

"I never said any such thing. Stop imagining things, Carl. Now let's all have tea. I'll fix it—stay out of the kitchen everybody—I know where things are. It's been awfully nice of all of you to come and see me this afternoon."

And off she dashed to the kitchen. We looked at each other and sighed with relief, happy in the thought that Alice was to be spared for many more years to come.

"Well—that's Alice," said Grace.

Actresses of the old school were like that. They had to be. They were trained for a theater where they must be heard clear to the last row in the balcony. They had to have a surplus of energy, and an untamed and uncaged vitality. Today half of the young people in the theater can't be heard beyond the fifth row. They can, however, speak well and softly into a microphone—but they can't make the rafters ring in the grand manner of the actors of the old days. The stars of the 1900's knew nothing and cared less for the Stanislavsky method—all emotion within and nothing going over the footlights.

Theater was theater when I first came to New York, back in 1919. Naturally I took all my plays to Alice to read.

Her comment was, "For what you've done—they are all right, I suppose. But I don't see a single part in any of your plays for me."

"I'll write one especially for you," I said.

Alice smiled happily. "That's what Grace Livingston Furniss did. She wrote *Mrs. Jack*, my first starring vehicle, with me in mind. You must meet Grace. It was a wonderful part—a breezy Middle Western woman. Douglas Fairbanks played a minor part—but we had to let him go. He was always breaking things."

Tailoring a play to a star would be, I felt, a good experience for me. I should be able to learn a lot about playwriting.

"What kind of a part would you like to play?" I asked.

Alice thought a moment. "Chief Justice Holmes has told me I'd have made an ideal senator's wife, as I never forget a face, and even though some people may get mad at me when I tell them what they should do, they never stay mad long when they find out I am right. I'll be a senator's wife—say from Indiana—that's where Eugene V. Debs was born, too."

"Oh, the Socialist who's always getting into trouble."

"He's not a Socialist. He came from Terre Haute. Am I a Socialist because I come from Indiana, too? Don't make those silly remarks, Carl," she said, loyal as always to her friends.

Alice had me meet Grace Furniss, as she felt we could talk over the play together. Grace had written a great many plays that had been successful on Broadway. She was still writing plays, although at this time she must have been somewhere in her sixties. Certainly she still dressed in the style of the 1900's, and ignored changes in fashions. She always wore a long dress clear to the floor, even when skirts kept getting higher and higher. Her collar came close about her neck, and she had long, flowing sleeves with white lace cuffs.

On her bosom was plastered a watch. She was the perfect picture of the proper gentlewoman of days gone by, the well beloved great-aunt. She'd sit quietly erect in her chair, her hands folded in her lap, and you felt on first meeting her that you must watch your language and not say anything shocking. But she didn't quite fulfill the promise of a respectable propriety. She knew all the very latest slang—and when she spoke, you heard words and expressions that your great-aunt would never have understood.

She had a home in Rye, and invited me to come and spend a week end with her, so that we could talk over the play I had in mind for Alice. After breakfast on the Sunday morning of my visit, Grace said, "Glick, old boy—will you do this flapper a favor?"

"Yes, ma'am," I answered.

"Go out on the porch—put your big feet on the rail—smoke a cigarette. I want my nosy neighbors to know that, bigawd, last night I had a man in the house!"

"Yes, ma'am," I said, and did as I was told.

When the first act of my play for Alice was completed, I took it to her to read. It was a mistake. She wanted lines taken from other characters and given to her to speak. So I cut and rewrote. More changes. More cuts. I could plainly see that I'd never get beyond writing the first act, and probably spend a lifetime at that. I became desperate. It was a tailor-made play, all right, but it was being so changed, so cut, so altered that, like a piece of cloth being slashed to bits, nothing was left but a leading role for Alice. I was ready—and rightly—to drop my immortal words into the waste-paper basket.

Rather angrily I said to Alice, "This play doesn't jell properly. But I have an idea for another play for you. Stunning—and what a role for you! The scene is laid in a deaf-and-dumb asylum. You're the matron—and the only person in the play who has a line of dialogue."

"Wonderful," exclaimed Alice, and wasn't angry, as I thought she would be. "That's exactly the sort of role I've always wanted to play. And here's the title: *I'll Do All the Talking.*"

There was never any use trying to get ahead of Alice.

Every summer she'd go to Gloucester, Massachusetts, which was a very popular resort with Alice and her friends. Grace Filkins used to go there, too. When she had been leading lady years before in a play with Henry Miller, Grace had worn a riding habit. She kept it, for despite her years, having a neat, trim figure, she looked marvelous in a riding habit. At Gloucester, by the sea, there were no riding horses, and even if there had been Grace didn't ride, never had, and never intended to. But mornings she'd put on the riding habit and stride up and down the hotel veranda, slapping her legs with her riding crop and looking very chic and smart indeed.

But came the day when Alice couldn't stand this offstage performance any longer. In a loud voice that could be heard by everybody on the veranda, Alice said, "Listen, Grace, all you need to make the illusion complete is the smell of manure about you."

For two days they didn't speak; and then one evening, playing bridge, they drew each other as partners. Alice trumped Grace's ace, and Grace now was happy. She had a great deal to say in reminding Alice of her error.

One day on Broadway I ran into Grace. She was rehearsing in a new play at the time. But this morning she was furious about something.

"What's the trouble?" I asked.

"Am I a bitch?" she exclaimed. "What is a bitch? As the wife of

Rear Admiral Marix I moved in the best social circles in Washington, London, and all over the world, and I've never before in my life heard the word used. What is a bitch?"

"It's something applied to—" I started to explain properly.

"Don't tell me!" she stormed. "I'm a lady—and I do not wish to know. Am I a bitch?"

"Certainly not. How could you be? Why do you ask?"

Grace named a certain actress in the company and said, "This morning at rehearsal she called me a bitch! Me—of all people. As the wife of Rear Admiral Marix I never in the fashionable circles I moved in heard the word used. Certainly I never used such language. I'm a lady—and my friends are all ladies. And that woman had the impertinence to call me a bitch!"

"Shocking," I said. "I'm horrified. What did you do?"

"I looked her straight in the eyes and said, 'You're a goddamn slut!' " Grace replied emphatically.

When I told Alice this story, she replied, "I'm surprised that Grace would use that word in the presence of a clean-minded young man like you. We'll have to go to the opening night and see who spoke the truth."

It was great fun and excitement, going to the theater with Alice, especially when one of her dearest friends was either starring in the play or playing a leading role. Alice always liked to sit in a box. She'd warn me several times that the curtain was to be at eight-thirty and for me to be on hand at least twenty minutes before curtain time. I'd be punctual, too, as would her other guests. But Alice wouldn't arrive until late, just in time to make an effective entrance before the curtain rose.

She would seat her guests, but just as soon as we were comfortable, she'd decide she didn't like the arrangement, and would have us all change. That wouldn't satisfy her, either, and we'd all have to move again. Then she'd see some friends in the audience. She'd call to them by name, wave her hand in greeting, and blow them a kiss. Then she'd rearrange once more the seating of her guests in the box. By that time half the audience was watching this performance. And Alice kept it up until the curtain rose, and only then could we sit back and relax after our setting-up exercises.

On the night that Grace made her first entrance, looking lovely and sparkling, Alice leaned forward and started the applause, saying in a loud voice that carried over the footlights, "Doesn't she look young!"

Grace acknowledged the compliment with a brave smile and a wave of her hand, with her thumb lightly brushing her nose in passing.

Once at midnight the telephone rang. It was Alice, very excited.

"I've just received a telegram from the Players Club," she said. "They are doing as their spring revival *The Way of the World* by Congreve, and want me for the role of Lady Wishfort. You've been to college—is it a good part?"

"The best in the play, I think," I answered.

"But Lady Wishfort! What does it mean?"

"Just what it says," I answered. "Wish for it."

"Wish for what? Fame? Money? Social position? What? You're a college graduate, and should know. Why are you pretending you don't? Be specific. What does she wish for?"

"Don't be naive, Alice," I said. "You're a grown woman."

"But why don't you answer me? What good was your college education if you can't explain these things? Lady Wishfort. Wish what? I don't understand."

"I can't explain over the phone," I answered. "I'll come over tomorrow and bring you a book entitled *What Every Young Girl Should Know*."

There was an ominous pause.

"Oh," said Alice finally. "Why didn't you say so in the first place? But I don't need that book. I've read it. Bring me a copy of the play, and if it's as good a part as you say it is—I'll play it—no matter what!"

And she did, too. I held the playbook for her while she learned her lines. She had at least eight different interpretations for each speech, and spent hours trying to determine which reading was the most effective. There was one line, however, that bothered her. It was when Lady Wishfort, in a haughty moment, said testily, "What —am I to be a receptacle for a decayed pimp?"

"Now how am I—of all people—going to read that line?" she stormed. "What's a pimp? Are you a pimp? Don't tell me. It's better I didn't know. Then I can say the line without blushing."

On the opening night, when she delivered that speech with a perfect air of outraged innocence, the audience roared. Her technique in such matters was perfect.

Finally, through the people Alice had introduced me to, I had a play accepted for production on Broadway. It was a melodrama entitled *The Devil's Host*. It had, however, been produced in England previously, being the first time an American's first play received its *première* in London rather than in New York. It ran almost three months in London. It might have been a success here, too, if on the opening night there hadn't happened one of those unforeseen tragic mishaps over which no playwright has control.

It was a raw evening in November, but as I sneaked into the theater to see my brain child born into the world, beads of perspiration stood out on my forehead, and my face was drawn and tense.

I found a seat in the top balcony where I could suffer in silence. The curtain rose and the play was on. I took a long, deep breath. The plot concerned a man who posed as the devil, but really had a heart of gold and was a true friend of the people. He was scheming to expose a corrupt politician and an even more corrupt banker. The actor playing the banker was an impressive, heavy-set man weighing well over two hundred pounds. He had a deep, booming voice, and looked more like a prosperous Wall Street banker than J. Pierpont Morgan himself.

In the crucial moment of the play the devil, to win his point, accuses the banker of having an illegitimate daughter.

The banker was supposed to thunder back in an outraged booming voice, "Are you trying to insinuate I am the father of that girl?"

It was carefully rehearsed—as this was a tense moment in the play—that then the devil would pause, long and ominously, and reply softly, "Yes."

Everything was going well up to this point, and I was beginning to relax. The devil made his accusation. But then the deep bass voice of the banker echoed to the rafters as he cried, "Are you trying to insinuate I am the *mother* of that girl!"

The audience relaxed and howled with laughter. What could the devil do but say, "Don't you mean the father?" Again the audience howled.

I stumbled out of the theater and hurried to the nearest speakeasy. Later I was told that during the rest of the play—and it was a serious drama, remember that—every time the banker opened his mouth to speak, the audience remembered and laughed. The play stumbled along on Broadway for four short weeks, and then closed. It was my first and last play to be produced on Broadway.

One Saturday morning while the play was still open I received a hurried call from the producer. One of the actors was ill and couldn't play in the matinee performance. There was no understudy. Now, since I had once been an actor, had written the play, and obviously knew all the lines—why shouldn't I play the role for the matinee performance? I said I would. It was a rare opportunity. Perhaps I was destined after all to become an actor. Perhaps the Shuberts would see me that afternoon, offer me other parts, and in time I might become a star on Broadway, acting in many plays of my own writing.

Now, as it happened I opened the play. Immediately upon the rise of the curtain, the butler ushered me into the room, saying, "This way, sir."

I stepped upon the stage, and in a well-modulated voice said, "Thank you."

From the darkened auditorium came the loud voice of Alice Fischer, gasping, "It's Carl!"

I hadn't had time to tell her, and she had come to the play that afternoon bringing with her Grace Furniss. Every line went completely out of my head, I was so startled. I turned my back to the audience and said to George Le Soir, a fine, seasoned actor who was playing the butler, "What do I say now?"

He quickly gave me the cue, and somehow I managed to get through the first short scene. I was playing the part of a successful novelist, one who had displayed great promise in his youth, but now had sold his soul for money and was writing for the slick magazines and the movies. The next character to appear upon the stage was my old boyhood sweetheart whom I hadn't seen in years. She, too, had once showed great promise as an actress, but like myself had also sold her soul for filthy lucre. And now here we were once again, reminding each other of our failure and having one of those touching "do you remember when we were young and gay, Maggie?" scenes.

Now, even though I had written the play, and was supposed to know all the lines, during this scene I couldn't for the life of me remember who said what to whom. I started in, and began to say all the lines in the play—her lines as well as my own. They all sounded alike anyway. She would start to interrupt me, but fearful lest I was not saying the right line, on I went. It was a monologue, while she stood there gasping. We might have gone on forever in this manner if the stage manager, sensing our predicament, had not thrust onto the stage the next character, and I faded into the background. The play went on. But I didn't remember the business. All that afternoon the actors would whisper to me when I got in their way, "Move downstage left." I was confused. I moved over right. It was a free-for-all.

When it was finally over, Alice came backstage with Grace.

"Well," she said, "so you're an actor now!"

I explained what had happened, and asked her how I did.

One of Alice's admirable qualities was her truthfulness. "Let's not discuss it," she said. "But I had the strange feeling this afternoon that Edwin Booth was turning over in his grave."

Grace, hoping to cheer me up, added hastily, "But I thought the play had merits."

The truth didn't hurt as much as it should, and I felt I might as well be honest with myself and admit that I wasn't destined to be an actor. Yet I had achieved one of my youthful ambitions. I had acted on Broadway in a play of my own writing. That was triumph enough for one lifetime. Sagerson's prophecy had come true. I had had a play produced—but it hadn't made me happy.

Every so often I read in the newspapers about a super-super benefit for some charity being held at Madison Square Garden, at which the stars of the screen, stage, and radio make personal appearances. I don't know what goes on backstage when they all get together, but it probably isn't much different from the time Alice had a hand in managing and running such a benefit performance.

The winter of 1922 hadn't been too good a year theatrically for many of the stars. So they decided to give a benefit performance as a memorial tribute to Mrs. James Speyer, the wife of the banker, who had been a great friend to them all. Mrs. Speyer had founded and built the Ellin Prince Speyer Hospital for Animals on Lafayette Street. So why not give a gala performance, in which they could all appear once again and at the same time raise money for homeless cats and dogs? Elizabeth Marbury, the celebrated play broker, was made chairman, and her assisting committee was an imposing list of names of all the celebrated actresses of the day.

Alice phoned me, saying, "I'm going to make you one of the assistant stage managers. You've got to drop everything and help us out."

"What do I do?" I asked.

"See that everything runs smoothly. Help keep order backstage, and see that everyone is on time. Tell them what to do—none of them will know."

"You mean," I gasped, "that I've got to boss around such stars as Viola Allen, Grace George, Blanche Bates, Julia Arthur, Elsie Janis, Margaret Anglin, and—and—"

"That's it, exactly!" said Alice.

Nervously I took on the responsibility. On the afternoon of the benefit, which was given at the Shubert Theatre, the house was packed. Boxes sold for $200, and the seats in the orchestra were priced at $5, which was high for those days. Leaders of New York Society were on hand, many of whom had gladly consented to serve as patronesses. It was an imposing list of names—both behind the footlights and in the audience.

Shortly before the curtain rose, Elizabeth Marbury stormed into the theater. She was a huge woman, as round as a barrel, and always carried a cane.

"Glick," she snapped. "Get me a chair—a solid one that I won't break. Put it there," indicating a spot in the wings. She planked herself down, pounded the floor with her cane, and ordered, "Now Glick—tell these goddamn amateurs to begin on time!"

Of course, everyone couldn't be given a leading role in the various sketches. So very cleverly someone thought up the idea that a sort of playlet should be written, entitled *After the Benefit*. It would be a scene in a drawing room, where Elsie DeWolfe, Viola Allen, Blanche Bates, and Julia Arthur would act as hostesses. Robert Warwick would be the butler, and announce each star separately as they came in—hoping the audience would applaud.

"They will, too," said Alice. "Plant me in one of the boxes, and I'll make comments and start the applause."

It turned out happily, for most of the stars submitted to Alice exactly what they wanted said about themselves, and Alice very generously said what they wanted. The big moment of the party onstage was to be that, when the stars were all asembled, Emma Calvé from the Metropolitan Opera would be announced, sweep into the drawing room, sing a song, and bring down the curtain.

Madame Calvé arrived at the theater early, with her accompanist, her manager, her maid, her chauffeur, her secretary, and a few friends. She was given the star's dressing room, and there she held court. But as the afternoon dragged on, and she was kept waiting, she became nervous. Someone hurried to Elizabeth Marbury and reported, "Calvé is getting impatient. It's now after four o'clock —and she wants to know when she's got to go on. If it isn't soon, she may get temperamental and go home!"

Amelia Bingham was standing near by with a huge bouquet of red roses that an admirer had sent her. Elizabeth Marbury grabbed the flowers from Amelia Bingham and thrust them at me.

"Here, Glick—take these rosebuds to Calvé. Tell her—and don't bother being polite—that Mrs. Vanderbilt raised them in her own hothouse. Tell Calvé that Mrs. Vanderbilt came this afternoon just to hear her sing—and she won't leave the theater until the last high note. Tell Calvé that—that should keep that opera bird quiet."

I hastened to the dressing room, and as politely as I could, presented the flowers to Madame Calvé with the compliments of Mrs. Vanderbilt, and added, "She is waiting just to hear you sing, and hopes you aren't leaving."

"Oh-la-la," smiled Calvé. "Dear Mrs. Vanderbilt! Tell her I have no intention of leaving!"

One of Mr. Speyer's secretaries had an autograph album that the stars were all to sign, and then it was to be auctioned off. As I remember, the highest bidder that afternoon paid one thousand dollars for the book.

As the secretary was collecting autographs, she came up to me. "Who is that very handsome young man over there?" she asked. "I can't place him—but he must be a well-known actor, or he wouldn't be here."

I couldn't place him, either, so to be on the safe side I suggested that he be asked to sign the book anyway. He smilingly consented and signed. The secretary showed me his signature.

"Who is he?" she said. "I don't recognize the name."

I didn't, either, so I inquired. The answer was simple. He was Madame Calvé's chauffeur.

When the final curtain fell and everybody had congratulated everybody else and said, "We must have another benefit soon," Elizabeth Marbury asked me if I had enjoyed myself.

"I've directed amateurs in Little Theaters," I said, somewhat exhausted. "But it's been nothing to equal this."

"Didn't I tell you they were amateurs!" she replied coldly, as if I had dared to doubt her word, and then stalked away.

She was right, of course. I felt that the only difference between the dowagers of Waterloo who acted for fun, and the stars of the theater, was that they acted, and not only had fun but got paid for it, and very well indeed, too.

Of course I kept on writing plays, but nobody seemed to want them. There's a trunkful in the basement at the moment. And there they'd better stay, mementos of a stage-struck youthful playwright who never got anywhere in the professional theater.

Then one summer day in 1923 came a letter from Dr. George Reynolds, my former teacher at the University of Montana. He was chairman of the English Department at the University of Colorado at that time, and he asked me if I would be interested in teaching for one year. He made it quite plain that it was only for one year, and that I would be substituting for Professor Francis Wolle, who was taking his sabbatical. It would be a refreshing experience, I thought, and since it was only for one year—well, I might have fun. Perhaps in my spare time I might start a novel—*the* great American novel. I was all of thirty-three years old at the time— but hopeful, even if still a trifle damp behind the ears.

When I bade good-by to Alice Fischer, I told her how much I felt in her debt, and that she had done many kindnesses for me that I could never repay in kind.

"I don't expect you to," she answered. "When I came to New York years ago, Frank Mayo, Joseph Jefferson, and many others were kind to me. How could I repay them? I couldn't. So my philosophy is, pass along kindness, encouragement, and help to others. When you go to Colorado, do what you can for the students you meet. Help others younger than yourself—and don't expect payment in kind. When they are older and have succeeded, in turn they'll help the youth they know. Good luck in Colorado—and write often."

So I borrowed some money, bought a new suit, and took the train to Colorado.

12

✣

OH, PROFESSOR!

NOT long after my arrival at the University of Colorado I received a note from the dean asking that I drop into his office. I had no idea what he wanted. Perhaps he was going to compliment me on my teaching. In that event I was all prepared to be very modest and humble and say that his compliments were totally undeserved.

Dean Hellems was one of my favorite persons. He had a droll sense of humor and a great understanding of human virtues and frailties. It was necessary in his position, dealing sternly with students on the one hand and diplomatically with faculty members on the other. Above his desk he kept a pair of fencing foils, and it was well known about the campus that he knew how to use them, too.

So that morning I dropped into his office, smiling and at ease, for it was always a great pleasure to chat with Dean Hellems.

But he wasn't smiling as he motioned me to a seat and said abruptly, "I hear you've been drinking with the students."

"Yes, sir," I replied truthfully. "But it's pretty bad stuff, and I don't recommend it."

Now, this was during prohibition, and bootleggers were thicker on the campus than faculty wives.

Dean Hellems glared at me a moment, then asked, "Don't you

know faculty members aren't supposed to drink with the students?"

"I've heard rumors it isn't a common practice," I replied.

"Then why do you do it?"

"I was told in New York that if a man in Colorado offered me a drink and I refused—I'd be shot. I've been acting in self-defense."

"A mistaken notion," he mumbled. "Possibly true in the old, untamed days of the Wild West. But the custom—while a good one—has long since been abolished."

Then he softened a bit and added, "I like a glass of sherry myself, now and then. And should you want a drink occasionally, who am I to deny you that privilege? However, in the future, please drink only with members of the faculty."

"Which faculty members?" I asked.

He dismissed me with a gesture.

After all, what drinking I had done was in the nature of a minor extracurricular activity. Now and then some of us would get a jug of red wine, drive up the canyon, build a fire, and then sit around discussing literature and the finer things of life. It became a sort of informal classroom. I learned a great deal from my students.

It was one of the happiest years of my life. The faculty were friendly. The students were friendly. And what a joy it was to be once again with my good friends, Dr. and Mrs. Reynolds. Since I'd be packing my bags when spring came and going back to New York, why not have fun while fun was to be had?

Then one April morning Dean Hellems called me once again into his office. I was shaking in my boots—for I wondered what now?

He went straight to the point. "President Norlin and I have been talking about you," he said.

("Oh-oh," I thought to myself. "He's heard about that party up the canyon last Saturday night. But so what? I'll be leaving in another month.")

"We love this University. It means a great deal to both of us. We came here years ago as young men."

("I'd better start packing right now," I thought.)

"We've given our best and devoted our lives and our efforts to this University. We've seen it grow from a few buildings to the present beautiful campus."

("If I pack this afternoon," I thought, "I can catch a train out tomorrow.")

"To us this University is like a cathedral!"

("I'd better take the first train out this afternoon—and let someone pack my stuff and send it after me!")

"But a cathedral is not complete unless it has a gargoyle. So the president and I have decided to ask you back for another year!"

There were tears in my eyes as I thanked him. It was one of the nicest compliments I've ever had paid me. And I vowed, then and there, that next year I'd not do any more drinking of bad liquor with the students.

But should I remain another year? I had had a truly wonderful time—but hadn't written a single line on the great American novel. Nor had I saved much money. There was but one thing to do— go and have Mrs. Hayden tell the cards for me, and see what she had to say.

Mrs. Hayden was a little old lady close to eighty. She never, to my knowledge, set foot upon the campus, yet she knew more about what was going on than the Dean of Men and the Dean of Women combined. If you mentioned her name at a faculty party, some of the wives lifted an eyebrow and claimed they'd never heard of her. Having your fortune told with cards was not considered a proper academic pastime. Yet Mrs. Hayden had a certain literary heritage. For she was born in England, and when she was a little girl Charles Dickens had patted her on the head and given her a shilling. She always kept it as a lucky piece.

She had been a nurse in a hospital in London when she met and married Mr. Hayden, who was valet to the King's Messenger. Coming to this country, they settled in Boulder and bought a home at the foot of the mountains, a short walk from the campus. Their living room was a bit of old England. There were portraits of Queen Victoria and Edward, Prince of Wales, draped with a British flag. Mrs. Hayden loved her home and saw no reason to venture into town. She was much too busy telling fortunes, anyway. And why should she go out when people came to her?

The only times she did leave her home were when she had invitations from some of the society dowagers of Denver who wanted their fortunes told. They'd send a limousine with a chauffeur for Mrs. Hayden. She'd put on her Sunday best, a rustling black silk gown in the Victorian style, with a brooch over her heart that she said Edward had given her when he was Prince of Wales. She always had a wonderful time in Denver, with the flower of Denver's society, telling their fortunes and entertaining them with choice bits of gossip about the royal family and the dear Queen Victoria.

But usually she sat around home in a faded kimono, a lace cap on her head, and in winter a knitted shawl on her shoulders. You'd cut the cards, make a wish, and then Mrs. Hayden would tell you exactly what you wanted to know. As you left you'd lay a quarter—no more, no less—on the mantel beneath the smiling portrait of the Queen.

I grew very fond of Mrs. Hayden, and we became great friends. Sometimes on Sunday evenings, after vesper service at the University, I'd ramble out past the cemetery to see the Haydens. She never told fortunes, however, on Sunday. So on these occasions I'd go around to the back of the house and rap on the kitchen door. Then we'd sit around the stove, and Mr. Hayden would give me a glass of his well aged, homemade dandelion wine. He was Sheriff of Boulder County at the time, and the wine he made was much better than the raw stuff we got from the bootleggers.

Once, growing bold on the heady wine, I asked Mrs. Hayden if she believed the fortunes she told people.

"Sometimes it's quite uncanny what the cards say," she replied, with a merry twinkle in her bright eyes. "Sometimes I tell the truth as I know it—and sometimes the most unexpected things just pop out. Tell me, do you know ——— ?" and she mentioned the name of a student.

I did. Jennie was in one of my classes.

"She's coming to see me Tuesday. Tell me, what do you know about her?"

"Quite a bit," I replied, and gave Mrs. Hayden the complete low-down on Jennie.

And that was how I became one of Mrs. Hayden's most trusted agents. On Sunday evenings she'd tell me who was coming to have their fortunes told the following week, and I'd tell her all I knew about them. While I don't make a general practice of gossiping about people, this, I felt, was different. It served a good purpose. So I'd let Mrs. Hayden know what boy was in love with which girl —and what girl had a crush on which boy. I'd also tell her what, to the best of my knowledge, various students would receive as their grades in the courses they were taking. I often made a point of finding out from other professors. It's a common enough practice for instructors to discuss among themselves the standing of the students.

Naturally, I never let people know I visited with the Haydens on Sunday evenings, and that now and then I sent her a special delivery letter containing bits of information she might find of value. Openly, of course, I scoffed at fortunetellers and said it was all nonsense.

One student, offended at my attitude, said, "I really think you're wrong, Professor. I believe there's something in it. There's a fortuneteller here in town—a Mrs. Hayden. She's positively uncanny. Why, she told me two weeks before final examinations that I was going to pass your course and gave me almost exactly the grade you gave me. You should go out and see her. I'm certain you'd change your mind."

I wasn't her only agent, of course. She had others about town, but I covered the University. While I was never certain just who these other agents were, I did suspect a respectable matron in town who knew everything that went on in Boulder society. Then, too, Mr. Hayden, in his office of Sheriff, was a great help.

My conscience never hurt me a bit. With Mrs. Hayden reading the cards was a hobby, a pastime, an art, and not a commercial project. She loved people and she liked to have them come to see her.

She once said, "I try to do good for people. Sometimes they'll believe the cards and take what advice I have to give them much quicker than they will accept the advice of friends or relatives."

I know this to be true. There was the case of a husband and wife about to separate. It would have been most tragic if they had. I happened to know some of the story and confided it to Mrs Hayden. Then one day, talking with the wife, I remarked that fortunetelling was nonsense, but said that I had heard of a Mrs. Hayden who lived right here in Boulder—and that some of my students claimed that she had told them the most amazing things. So that week the wife went to see Mrs. Hayden.

Afterwards the wife said to me, "You must never make fun of fortunetellers. Mrs. Hayden is most uncanny! She knew all about my husband and myself—and she was right in that it's partly my fault we don't get along. I'm going to take her advice. It would be a great mistake if I broke up our home."

Matters were patched up, and the last I heard of this couple, they were living happily ever after.

Mrs. Hayden straightened out a number of students who might have gone off the deep end if they hadn't taken the advice she gave them. Despite the fact that some disbelievers frowned upon her, she was one of the greatest forces for good that I knew in University circles. A friendly, bubbly, gracious little old lady. What fun she had!

So, when Dean Hellems asked me back for the second year, I went to see Mrs. Hayden. Should I stay another year, or should I go back to New York?

She read the cards and told me to stay another year. Then she looked very grave and said, "However, there's a lot of gossip around you. People talk about you—much too much. You drink with the students. It's here in the cards. And here's the card that advises you to be more cautious. If you want a little nip before dinner, that's all right. Here's a card saying you are about to receive a present."

"Does it say from whom?" I asked.

"Yes. It's from Mr. Hayden. He has a bottle of his dandelion wine you are to take home with you. But you aren't to give this to the students. It's much too good for them. Have it yourself. And when this is gone, come back—and Mr. Hayden will give you another bottle."

The next September I was on the train, returning for my second year at the University of Colorado. I was very happy about it. In the morning the train would pull into Denver, and then I'd jog on to Boulder. It was, in a sense, my last night of freedom. Once in Boulder I would be called "Professor" and expected to be upon my good behavior.

Seated next to me in the observation car that evening was a very pretty young girl. She looked at me quizzically, as if expecting me to start the conversational ball rolling. I did. I said something brilliant about the weather. She agreed that it had been a lovely day.

She was very charming; and masculine vanity being what it is, I thought I'd tell her something about myself. But I decided not to pull the "I'm a writer" gag, and certainly not tell her I was that most prosaic and conventional of persons, a college professor. She was so lovely to look at that she deserved something much more glamorous and exciting.

So I thought up a beautiful story. I had a long, long journey ahead of me. I was bound for China as a medical missionary.

"It must be most interesting work," she murmured.

It was, I told her. Becoming inspired, I let my fancy roam. I told her of the many sacrifices I was making. Had I remained in this country, I could have secured a most lucrative post in a large hospital. But no—I didn't care for money. What inspired me was the thought of giving my life for others, of doing good for those less fortunate than myself. That was why I was leaving all behind me and going to faraway China, with banners waving and a heart of gold.

"How truly wonderful you are," she murmured from time to time, in the moments that I paused for breath. "You are truly courageous. Truly noble!"

I was in a fine glow. I had her practically in tears. Finally she rose, and smiled.

"It's high time for me to turn in," she said. "This winter at the University of Colorado I am certainly going to take a course with you, Professor Glick. And I expect to pass, too. Be good, Professor. Be very, very good!"

She did take a course, too. It was called Continental Fiction. What wonderful papers she wrote, even though now and then she made an absurdly far-fetched statement. In her paper on Flaubert's *Madame Bovary* she said, "The great trouble with Emma was she romanticized too much about herself and didn't always tell the truth. But then she had never met a missionary to China."

In her paper on Dostoevsky's *Crime and Punishment* she said, "The author of this well-written novel has as his thesis, 'Is murder justifiable?' In China, I understand, missionaries are often murdered for no reason whatsoever. Is this true, Professor?"

It was blackmail! She passed the course, and with a very good grade indeed.

My Continental Fiction course included the great Russian novels of Turgenev, Tolstoy, and Dostoevsky. In preparing the students for their reading of these writers, I worked up a lecture on the characteristics of the Russian people, and hoped to explain why they were like what they were and why they wrote such long-winded novels. I had some ten characteristics, all neatly numbered.

As I delivered the lecture the students took notes solemnly and religiously. But one student in the back row laughed at everything I said, and didn't write down a word. When the session was over, I signaled for her to speak to me after class.

"What's so funny about this lecture I've just been giving on the Russians?" I asked, belligerently.

She smiled sweetly and replied, "I'm Russian!"

Now culture does not flourish only on college campuses. In Denver the young ladies of the Junior League, besides their usual round of dances, tea parties, and debutante receptions, devoted some of their leisure time to improving their minds. Once a month they gave a luncheon, with a speaker to tell them all about some particular subject. Somehow by the grapevine they got word of my other course in Contemporary Literature, so I was tapped and invited to deliver a talk on the present-day trends of modern writing. But three days before the appointed day I received a post card, saying that my topic was Contemporary Russian Literature.

Of all things! This was in 1925. At that time the Revolution was still popular in Russia, hence there was even less Russian literature being translated and published in this country than there is today. New Russian novels? In my ignorance I simply didn't know of a single one.

But, since the ladies expected from me a talk on Contemporary Russian Literature, I'd do my best. First of all, I briefly sketched the background of the classical Russian novelists and spoke of Tolstoy, Turgenev, Dostoevsky, and Gogol. Then, warming up, I spoke about the great poet Anna Sergyevna (a name I had gotten from Turgenev's *Fathers and Sons*—see page 123). She was, I told the young ladies, a writer of free verse. I read aloud some of her most famous poems, which I had written the night before, in-

spired by a bottle of Mr. Hayden's dandelion wine. And I pointed
out that Anna's verse was rugged, passionate, and full of the sad,
sad undertones of suffering Mother Russia.

One of the poems went like this:

> *I am the earth,*
> *Parched and thirsting.*
> *I groan and bear the wheat*
> *Stirring uneasily within me.*
> *Over me pass the dark storm clouds.*
> *Rain falls.*
> *I seek surcease to my sorrow and suffering*
> *From their outpourings.*

Intense, passionate stuff like that. The young ladies loved the
poems, and I wish I had written more. But my *pièce de résistance*
was the great realistic novel *Submerged Souls*, by Serge Oblasky.
I explained that it was impossible for me to outline the plot in
mixed company. It was the last word in realism, and was too, too
brutal. Serge left out nothing—nothing! I insinuated that this book
was probably the frankest discussion of sex ever written. Then
I asked for questions. Someone wanted to know what I thought of
Michael Arlen's *The Green Hat*, which was a popular book at
the time. At the luncheon they told me that my talk had been refreshing and stimulating, and they were all glad to know about the
Russians, which now they felt they must—simply must—read.

I went back to my chores at the University and forgot all about
Anna and Serge. But some time later I was in Denver again and
stopped in one of the leading bookstores. The manager came up
and wanted to know where he could get *Submerged Souls*, by Serge
Oblasky.

"I've looked in every publisher's catalogue, and can't find it listed
anywhere," he said.

"Why do you want that book?" I asked.

"You spoke about it at a luncheon—and everybody wants to read it," he answered. "I've got some fifty orders here. Where can I get it?"

I learned in Sunday School that if you tell one lie you have to tell another to cover up the first. So, bravely, I told the second lie. "I read it last summer in New York," I answered. "It was privately printed in England—by whom I don't know. But I'll write and try to find out for you."

"Please do," he answered. "It will certainly be a best-seller here in Denver."

I hurried from the store. As I was rambling down a side street, I paused in surprise. In the window of a pet shop some puppies were tumbling about. But standing in the doorway was a large, striking-looking, red-haired woman. We stared at each other in astonishment. She was just as surprised to see me in Denver as I was to see her.

"Migawd—Christine!" I exclaimed.

"Carl!" she cried.

Then she yelled into the store. "Pat—for the love of Mike—come quick and see who's here."

Out from the shop came her husband, Pat Barnum, a jovial, robust, handsome Irishman.

"What are you doing in Denver?" we all said to each other.

Pat indicated the pet shop. And when I told them I was teaching at the University of Colorado, they laughed, and seemed to think it was a good joke on me.

I had last seen Christine and Pat in New York. Together with Christine's mother, they ran a restaurant above the Provincetown Theater on MacDougal Street just off Washington Square in

Greenwich Village. This was in the 1920's, in the halcyon days
when the Village was really the Village, and acquiring the reputation for intellectual Bohemianism, low rents, starving artists, and
inexpensive tearooms. All the struggling young playwrights (among
them Eugene O'Neill), poets, novelists, and serious thinkers of
all sorts and descriptions flocked to Christine's. The dinner was
fifty cents. If some youthful genius didn't have the necessary cash,
Christine, in her big-hearted, generous way, would mutter, "Pay
me tomorrow when you sell a poem."

So few sold poems, so few ever paid Christine, that often she
had to borrow money to buy supplies for her restaurant for the next
day. But she was happy, having a glorious time feeding the hungry,
and it didn't matter—there'd always be a better tomorrow. Christine had had a colorful career.

She had been born in Denver. When she was eighteen, fired
by the zeal to save souls, she became a Salvation Army lass. Besides
beating the drum, she sang loudly and lustily in front of saloons,
pleading with the drunkards to reform and give up their evil ways.
One of the songs she sang went this way:

> There is a man in our town,
> His name is Mr. Brown.
> He prays for permission to vote for R-U-M.
> He helps to put the poison
> In his neighbor's C-U-P.
> And yet he has the breath
> To say, "I'm S-A-V-E-D."
>
> Glory, I am happy.
> Glory, I am free.
> Hallelujah, save the sinners.
> Make them just like me.

There is no record of just how many drunks she actually did save, but certainly she must have given many of the sinners food for thought, for she was a handsome, robust, lively young girl.

Then one day during a strike she heard a woman on a soap box exhorting the strikebreakers not to cross the picket line. It was a thrilling moment for Christine. She had never heard such a truly wonderful speaker. Christine was inspired by her fiery utterances. She spoke to the woman and asked if she could come and talk with her. The answer was yes.

And so Christine met Emma Goldman, the noted anarchist. Emma was a friendly, plump little woman. She looked more like a Middle Western housewife who spent most of her time in the kitchen getting dinner for a large family than she did the violent bomb thrower rumor said she was. But the only bombs that Emma Goldman ever threw were, said Christine, the bombs of intelligence and liberty. Emma needed a secretary, and Christine volunteered on the spot. Saving the soul of Mr. Brown, the capitalist, would be much more exciting than knocking the poison cup from the trembling hands of a repentant sinner. So for two years Christine traveled about the country with Emma Goldman, and probably received the most liberal education of any young girl of her generation.

Seeing Christine and Pat that day in Denver gave me an idea.

"Look, Christine," I said. "Many of the persons who used to come to your restaurant are now famous. The college girls are all reading and quoting Edna St. Vincent Millay. Everybody on the campus is discussing the writings of Sherwood Anderson, Floyd Dell, and Theodore Dreiser, and Eugene O'Neill is the literary god of the drama students. Why not come to the University some

evening and give a lecture? Tell us about these celebrities whom
you knew when they were young and struggling. It would be inspiring—and stimulating!"

Christine shuddered. "Me lecture?" she exclaimed in horror.
"Oh, migawd! Impossible—fantastic! You have your students. I
have my puppies. Never the twain shall meet!"

But Pat scratched his chin, gave me a wink, and looked thoughtful. It didn't take too much coaxing on his part to get Christine to
consent.

When I got back to the campus, I talked it over with some of
my colleagues. They, too, thought it was a fine idea. Every now
and then a lecturer would descend upon the University, and talk
to the students upon such topics as "The Solitude of the Soul" or
"My Visit to the Home of Longfellow" or some other such worthwhile and stimulating academic subject. Sometimes, even for these
lectures, attendance by the students was compulsory.

But we proposed to have a lecture course where attendance was
not required and we could hear topics discussed that were neither
academic nor too orthodox. Someone knew of a hypnotist in Denver
who might have a message. Then we learned that there was a man
living in solitude in the mountains who thought he was God. There
was also on the loose in Denver a Communist, and Communists
were rare birds in those days. We would sell season tickets, and
it would be most educational for the students.

Of course, Christine was the logical one to open the series, since
her topic was purely literary. We selected as a title for her lecture
"Wild Authors I Have Known."

But we had a problem. Should we rent a hall, or should we hold
the lecture right on the campus? The latter seemed the most
feasible. I spoke to Dr. Reynolds. He gave me a suspicious look,

grinned a bit, and referred me to Dean Hellems. Dean Hellems thought it over a moment, and said I'd better ask President Norlin.

President Norlin was a noted Greek scholar and had published several volumes of his own translations of obscure classic poets.

When I told him of our plan to bring Christine to the campus for a lecture, he asked, "What does she stand for?"

"Literature in the making," I assured him, and rattled off an imposing list of names of famous writers whom Christine had known intimately, among them Georgette Leblanc, the first wife of Maurice Maeterlinck.

"Maeterlinck is a great philosopher," said President Norlin. "I found his *The Life of the Bee* most impressive and very well written. It would be fine to have Christine tell the students about the home life of the Maeterlincks."

So that was settled. But Christine suddenly developed a severe attack of stage fright. She didn't mind acting in a play, she told us. In fact she had appeared in the original cast of O'Neill's *The Emperor Jones*. But the very thought of appearing in public without make-up and footlights gave her the jitters. Finally it was decided that I should sit with Christine on the platform, with notes in my hand, and ask her questions, and then she would tell us all. We rehearsed this as carefully as if it were a play.

Then Pat got temperamental. He wanted to perform, too. He could recite Poe's *The Raven* in a sepulchral voice with meaningful gestures, and could also give an amusing imitation of Caruso and Farrar singing the love duet from *Madam Butterfly*. To keep peace in the Barnum family, we decided that Pat should do his parlor stunts, too.

Our advance publicity was most effective. We advertised that Christine, dressed in her native Bohemian Greenwich Village costume, would give an informal talk which would be "cultural in the broadest sense of the word." She would give personal impressions of the many celebrities she knew, and since her talk was sponsored by "A Little Group of Serious Thinkers," the evening promised to be a rare treat for the campus intelligentsia. Tickets sold like hot cakes. On the night of the performance the Little Theater on the campus was packed with earnest, eager students and wistful faculty members.

We arranged a most artistic and appropriate setting. The deep blue cyclorama of the theater furnished the background, and on it hung a gay and colorful tapestry. In the center was a table covered with a Roman-striped shawl. On the table was a borrowed Russian samovar and several red candles, which we didn't dare light because of the fire laws. Over an imitation marble garden bench at one side was carelessly thrown a moth-eaten leopard's skin. There were two plain kitchen chairs beside the table, one for Christine and the other for me.

The performance began by Christine singing offstage the first few lines of her Salvation Army song. Then she walked upon the stage still singing, and the audience gasped.

Christine had spent many hours with her costume. Because of her flaming bobbed red hair, she had to dress properly. She wore a vivid batik blouse, a green velvet skirt, and around her middle, as a belt, she had wound an automobile tire chain. Her only jewelry was dozens of ten-cent-store bracelets, which clinked musically every time she made a gesture or raised or lowered her arms. When she first appeared, she was wearing a bawdy old-fashioned picture hat, on which drooped in an obscene manner a wilted ostrich feather.

As Christine sang the words of the chorus, "Glory, I am happy!

Glory, I am free! Hallelujah, save the sinners—make them just like me!" she threw the hat onto the marble bench. Then she ran her fingers threw her bobbed hair until it stood straight up on her head like a flaming red bush.

The audience, which had always seen lady lecturers formally clad in evening gowns, was so surprised that for a moment it sat stunned. Then some of the braver souls began to applaud and cheer, and Christine blew kisses to them, and sang the chorus all over again. From that moment on, the audience squirmed nervously in their seats. They didn't know just what might happen next.

When Christine finished singing, I strolled nonchalantly onto the stage, and greeted her as if I were coming into her restaurant for dinner.

"What's good tonight, Christine?" I asked.

"Same as usual," she answered. "I've got some tough Frank Harris with lemon sauce, some stewed Eugene O'Neill, a slice of Trotsky with onions, some tender portions of Edna St. Vincent Millay, and some pickled odds and ends left over from yesterday."

"Well—what about Eugene O'Neill?" I asked.

And into her first story plunged Christine. As she went on, telling of his early struggles, the time he disappeared for two days and was finally found beneath a mattress, and cast some not too delicate hints of his first love affairs, many of the admirers of Mr. O'Neill were frowning.

But not daunted, on we went. She told how Floyd Dell and his wife couldn't agree upon which they should have first, a baby or a bath tub. There was no compromise, as the baby and the bath tub both came at the same time, and were forever after that referred to as the "Dell twins."

She gave an imitation of Trotsky telephoning John D. Rockefeller and demanding finally and unequivocally that Rockefeller surrender immediately and send poor Trotsky by special messenger one bent dime.

Another imitation was that of Frank Harris, who was born in Kansas, coming in for dinner, peering through his monocle at the other diners, and deploring the lack of any hope whatsoever for poor, ignorant Americans.

She spoke of Edna St. Vincent Millay, and how she used to come to the restaurant for dinner wearing a kimono and slippers. She gave an impersonation of Edna phoning actors who were late to rehearsal for her "beautiful play," that made some of the college girls wonder how, on the one hand, anyone could write such beautiful poetry, and, on the other, speak so frankly to actors.

She sang the praises of Emma Goldman, and said that she was one of the first to start the fashion of bobbed hair, which had originated among the Communist gals in Russia.

As she would reach the climax of a story, she'd raise her arm. "Clink, clink, clink," would go the bracelets. Then she'd lower her arm. "Clink, clink, clink," and the bracelets would fall back into place.

Pat sang his duet, and the evening closed with his recitation of *The Raven*, the really literary highlight of the evening.

Opinion on the campus the next day was varied. Some of the students felt that they had had their illusions shattered. Others felt that they would like to go to Greenwich Village and be a part of the gay, sad life of starving authors. One faculty member contended that it was the most vulgar performance she had ever heard. A newspaper said, "From Christine's informal talk on 'Wild Authors I Have Known,' we are convinced there are such animals. The constant repetition of the 'light-fingered' characteristics of so many famous authors convinces us."

Christine had spoken of one well-known writer whom she had fed all one winter. But when his book was published and proved successful, he forgot completely to pay his board bill.

At class the next day some of the students asked me if all authors were really like that. I could only shake my head sadly, and reply, "I don't know. Cervantes went to jail, so did Bunyan, and there was a lot of gossip about Lord Byron. But perhaps we mustn't judge writers for what they are—but be grateful that what they wrote is beautiful, comforting, and highly moral."

After minor expenses were all paid, we gave Christine the rest, but saved out ten dollars to finance the next lecture. However, President Norlin called the sponsors into his office and gently remarked that from all reports the evening had been cultural in the broadest sense. But he suggested that perhaps we had better forget about the remainder of the planned lecture course. After all, he reminded us, the University had a bureau set up for the express purpose of bringing worthwhile speakers to the University, and any competition would be unfair to them.

So our Little Group of Serious Thinkers bought, with our ten dollars, a handsomely bound set of *Pilgrim's Progress*, and presented it to the University Library.

13

PROPER MODESTY

ALL this time, in my spare moments I kept on writing: stories, plays, and I even started a couple of novels, which I never finished. Remembering Sylvia, I wrote a series of stories about a two-hundred-pound burlesque queen—and sold them. With a grateful bow to Aunt America, I also did a series of stories about a gay lady who descended upon a small Middle Western town and upset a lot of apple carts. These were all accepted, too. But a lot of stories I wrote didn't sell, and ultimately found their resting place in my wastepaper basket. Holding down a job and trying to write, too, was something of a problem. I hoped that the day would come when I could lead the literary life with a vengeance. But in the meantime I kept on working and saving my money.

After my second year at the University of Colorado came an invitation to join the faculty at the University of Montana. I hailed the thought with delight. To return to Missoula, where I had had Gussie as my first student, would be an experience that I felt should not be missed. It would be like Conrad renewing his youth. I was thirty-five at the time.

But the University and the town had changed. A wave of morality had swept through Missoula in the years that I had been away. Front Street, where Gussie and her girls had lived, was now thoroughly respectable. It was a street of the homes of law-abiding citizens. And when I walked down the street and everyone called me "Professor," I saw no reason to blush or deny it.

But the winters were cold in Missoula. Snow on the sidewalks and the streets was often knee-deep. On early mornings when I walked from my apartment to the campus, I'd freeze the tip of my nose if I wasn't careful.

But I felt that if I had to have a red nose, I would rather it came from a bottle than the cold. One of the other young professors felt as I did about it. This was during Prohibition, and the bootleg liquor in and around Missoula was plain poison. I wasn't feeling well. Neither was Nat—so we both went to our doctors and got prescriptions filled. Between us we could obtain easily a pint a week from the downtown drugstore. We shared the bottles between us.

One particularly cold afternoon after our classes were over we were lamenting our lot. We wished that we were somewhere in the Sunny South. We took several more snorts, and then we had a brilliant idea. We sent a telegram to President Hamilton Holt of Rollins College, Winter Park, Florida.

The telegram said, "We are half frozen. The sun hasn't shown here for three months. Do you need two cold-blooded but warm-hearted young instructors on your faculty who look well in white flannels?"

We had a reply from President Holt the next morning. He said, "The trouble with my faculty is that they all think they look well in white flannels."

I had now had two years at Montana. We had built a Little Theater on the campus, the first in Montana. I could probably go on directing plays and giving courses in Sophomore Composition for the rest of my life. And by the time I got old and was ready to retire, I'd have long ago been snowed under by college themes. And then it would probably be too late to write the great American novel. So, when I received an invitation to go to San Antonio, Texas, and direct the newly organized Little Theater there, I didn't hesitate. I wired my acceptance.

In San Antonio I lived at the Menger Hotel. It had everything: an underground passage, a haunted room, a crocodile pool, a so-called "Latin Quarter" for artists, two patios luxuriant with palms, magnolias, flaming hibiscus, and flowers of all sorts, a kitchen from which came perfect dinners, and an old-world charm and friendliness that was unsurpassed.

I had an apartment in the Latin Quarter. Several artists had studios there, and so it became quite famous. Snoopy guests living at the hotel loved nothing better than to come to the Latin Quarter, which was in a wing separate from the rest of the hotel, and take a look at how the other half—the artists—lived. It was no uncommon occurrence to have strangers rap on my door at any time of the day and ask to see my studio apartment. At first it was somewhat pleasing to my vanity, but in time it became a plain nuisance. But how could I put a stop to these inquisitive persons?

One afternoon when I had just finished taking a cold shower, there was a rap on my door.

"Who is it?" I asked.

"We're from Indiana," said a thin, squeaky voice, "and we'd like to see your studio."

I had seen the speaker in the lobby with her friend. They were two elderly maiden ladies on a vacation, and not missing a single sight, including the Alamo and the missions.

"Are you certain you want to see my studio?" I asked.

"Yes—oh, yes!"

So, unclad as I was, I threw open the door and said pleasantly, "Come right in, ladies!"

They shrieked and fled. When they got safely back to the lobby, they must have told all their cronies of their horrible experience, for later that day when I strolled past the old ladies who sat in arm-chairs by the hour, I had some frigid but speculative looks. But I was never again bothered by such busybody sightseers.

The haunted room at the Menger fascinated me. It wasn't gen-erally known around the hotel which room it was, exactly. But there was one room which was always the last to be rented. Everyone who ever slept there complained. At about one o'clock or so in the morning they would be awakened by something dripping in the closet. It was said that a guest once hung himself there, and his ghost forever haunted the room.

I thought it would be an experience to sleep in that room, and if possible meet the ghost. From Edward, one of the Negro bell-hops, I obtained a bottle of bootleg *tequila,* a Mexican fire water but the best liquor obtainable in San Antonio during that Prohi-bition period. When Edward learned what I was planning, he strongly advised me against it. The thought frightened him. But he promised to come by, every half hour or so, to bring me ice and see if everything was going all right.

On his one-thirty tour of inspection, while I was fixing myself a drink and also getting one for Edward (who liked his liquor, too), from the closet there came the noise of something dripping. Drip—drip—drip! And growing louder. It was the ghost! Edward was so overcome that he fell to his knees and began to pray.

"Oh, Lord, forgive this poor sinner," he began.

"Forgive you for what?" I asked.

"I've drank your liquor when you wasn't around, Mr. Glick," he said. "I took four of your ties—but you hadn't worn them for a long time, and I didn't think you'd miss them. Forgive me, Mr. Ghost. If you spare me, I won't never again take a drop of liquor that ain't mine. I'se other sins, too. I ain't always been true to my wife. Spare me, Mr. Ghost, and I'll be a good boy from now on."

The dripping grew louder. I threw open the door of the closet. It was empty, as I know it would be. But the dripping continued.

"Hello, Mr. Ghost!" I said.

Edward grabbed my bottle of *tequila* and fled. Of course, there was no ghost. The answer to the mystery was simple. The bricks on the wall faced the hot sun during the day. But when they'd cool off at night, they'd make a cracking sound, exactly as if blood—in bucketfuls—was dripping upon the floor.

Knowing the answer, I went back to my own apartment. As I was going through the patio, there was Edward, passing the bottle around among some of the other bellboys.

"You took my liquor, Edward," I said, "and after you had promised the ghost."

"Yes, sir—but you saw me take it, and that's different," said Edward. "I'se just saving you, sir. If you drank with that ghost—no telling what might happen, sir." Then, hoping to make amends for helping himself to my liquor and ties, he said, "If I ever has a son, Mr. Glick, I'se sure going to name him after you."

"Are you expecting a son, Edward?" I asked.

"No, sir—but I'se going home right now and start working hard."

In the meantime I also was working hard with the Little Theater. We had no place to give our plays, save in rented halls and auditoriums, and each new auditorium to which we went proved more unsatisfactory than the last. When I brought up the idea of building our own theater, the question arose, where is the money to pay for it? I dug out of my files all that Donald Robertson had written about the need for a municipal theater, and presented the argument to the board of directors. Whatever one may say about the dowagers —and there's no denying that at times they can be trying and difficult—at least this can be said in their favor: when they see a vision and want something done—it's done. So, to the mayor went a committee of ladies, clad in their best. It resulted in the city government voting that bonds be issued and $104,000 be given to build a Little Theater in San Pedro Park. And built it was, the first city-built and city-owned Little Theater in the United States.

The formal opening was in January of 1930. Everything was in readiness on the night of the dress rehearsal of our first play in the new theater. The house was sold out. The opening night promised to be a social event, with the audience in evening dress. Many of the patron members were giving dinner parties before the play, and the cast and backstage staff were going to have a celebration of their own after the performance. I had gone home pretty much worn out, but I promised myself that I wouldn't get up the next morning until I felt like it, and would be thoroughly rested for the opening night's performance.

At nine o'clock the telephone rang. It was a call from the mayor's office. I was told that the theater couldn't open that night. The fire chief had not made his inspection yet and given his approval. I argued, what did it matter—that the theater was on the ground floor, with doors opening onto the sides, and everyone could get out in less time than it takes to tell it. But laws are laws. I started phoning the dowagers. They hurried to the mayor's office. Finally a compromise was reached.

That evening, as the audience drove up in their limousines and

Fords, there were a hook and ladder, a fire engine, and an emergency car and ambulance outside the theater. Backstage, getting completely in the way of the actors and the stage hands shifting scenery, were dozens of firemen, each clasping to his bosom, ready for any emergency, a baby fire extinguisher.

But everything went off smoothly, and all the precautions proved unnecessary. Who has ever heard of a Little Theater burning down, anyway?

I had had four very happy years, living in a fascinating hotel and a charming city. Then, too, I felt that I had saved up enough money to go to New York and do nothing else but write. If I lived modestly, I could get along in New York for a couple of years, at least. So I packed my trunk and departed.

Then came the Depression. One morning I woke up and discovered to my dismay that what few stocks and bonds I had were of value only as wallpaper. And the bank where I had my account was closed. I was broke. Even magazines weren't buying much in those days. Finally, however, I was given a job of sorts by the Emergency Work Bureau, and was sent to the Church of All Nations. Here I was assigned to the Chinese Athletic Club as their director—something that, even in my wildest dreams, I never thought I would be. But I became acquainted with the Chinese, and it opened up a new world to me.

I spent a year and a half at the Church of All Nations, and then came the chance to direct a Little Theater in Sarasota, Florida. There were no Chinese in Sarasota, not even a chop suey restaurant. I missed my Chinese friends, and their genial good humor and good manners.

One day I was invited to a children's party. When I got home, thinking things over, I wondered how a Chinese child would behave at such a party. The thought intrigued me. It would be a contrast of two different viewpoints. So I sat down and wrote a short story about a Chinese boy, "Li Tsang's First Party." To my surprise it sold, and a letter came, asking for more stories along this vein. Suddenly I realized that here was what I had been looking for all these years: a new field, and a new approach. Manna from heaven for a writer.

When I got back to New York that spring, I dusted off my typewriter and began writing stories about my Chinese friends. I even wrote a few articles concerning life in Chinatown. One was entitled "Number One Bad Boy," and explained the reasons why there is very little juvenile delinquency among the Chinese.

One of my Chinese friends read the article and came to me in great distress.

"You have ruined all of us!" he exclaimed. "Look—you say we are all well behaved. That we don't get arrested. You haven't told the truth."

I was greatly distressed. "What *is* the truth, then?" I asked.

"It's that we never get caught," he beamed. "But now what can we do? What fun can we have? We'll have to live up to your statements and be good boys. It's taken all the joy out of our lives."

"I'm sorry," I said. "I'll have the article suppressed."

"Oh, no—don't do that!" he exclaimed quickly. "The damage is done. We'll all try being good boys for a change. What are you writing next?"

Somehow the article came to the attention of State Senator Fred A. Young, Chairman of the New York Children's Court Jurisdiction and Juvenile Delinquency Commission. He raised a questioning eyebrow. Gathering together his committee, he went to Chinatown and held an investigation all his own. Later he wrote me, saying that the article had inspired the committee to visit Chinatown, and that he would like to include it in his report.

I showed this letter to my Chinese friend, saying, "See—State Senator Young finds that what I've said is true!"

"Yes, I know," he replied sadly. "But your article has made the Chinese in Chicago very angry."

"Now, why?" I sighed, in dismay.

"Because they haven't been investigated. But they are taking care of that themselves, and I'll let you know later what they find."

In time he showed me a newspaper clipping from Chicago that told how the Chinese there had made a thorough investigation and had discovered that juvenile delinquency among the Chinese was no problem at all to the Chicago police.

"They are now quite happy in Chicago," said my friend, in great glee. "The Chinese in Chicago have learned that they are no better and no worse than their cousins here in New York."

Then one day came a letter from William Poole, an editor at Whittlesey House, wanting to know if there was the possibility of my writing a book about the Chinese in America. He said he had read the article, and thought perhaps there might be a book that would be "sort of halfway between *The Importance of Living* by the Chinese philosopher Lin Yutang and *How to Win Friends and Influence People*," and would I be interested in talking with him about this? I was!

I talked it over with my Chinese friends.

Their reply was, "How can you write a book about us? We don't do anything interesting."

"You're just being modest," I said.

"But how will you go about it?"

"I'll ask questions, and you give me the answers," I said.

"Just an old busybody!"

"Exactly!"

And what an opportunity this was really to be a busybody! So I rambled around Chinatown, poked my nose into the affairs of my friends, and began asking questions.

Now, usually when I've said, "I'm a writer," people have broken down quickly and have told me all. But not the Chinese. They became very cagey. When I'd ask a question, they suddenly looked blank.

"I don't know the answer to that," they'd say.

But a week or so later would come a phone call. "Remember what you wanted to know? Well, I spoke to my elder brother. I think perhaps he knows the answer."

"Fine," I'd say. "I'd like to meet him."

"He's busy right now."

I was butting my head against a stone wall. But there was nothing I could do about it. I was rapidly acquiring a new virtue—patience.

Finally came the day when "elder brother" wasn't busy, and I was invited to Chinatown for dinner with him. As we sat dipping our chopsticks into dishes I had never tasted before, elder brother told me all I wanted to know, and more.

And at last, after this sort of thing had gone on for a couple of years, I had the information I wanted, and started writing the book. Then *Shake Hands With the Dragon* was finally published. But a sort of conspiracy of silence greeted the publication, from my Chinese friends.

Had I offended them? Actually, I had done a most impertinent thing. I had written up, in a factual book, stories of my Chinese friends. And while they had, in all friendliness and with great politeness, told me what I had wanted to know, it seemed plain that they didn't like the book. I wondered if I would ever dare set foot in Chinatown again.

One day one of my Chinese friends came to see me.

"My father is very angry with you," he said.

"Why?" I asked.

"Because you've written a book about us," he said soberly. "And the next time you are in Chinatown, he wants to see you."

His father was one of the most highly respected men in Chinatown, a most dignified gentleman of the old school. There seemed but one thing to do: go to see him and apologize. So off I went. When I saw him, he bowed politely. I didn't know whether to mention the book or let him say something about it. We talked about the weather, and other things, but not a word did he say concerning the book. As I was leaving, he handed me a large package, all wrapped up. It was, obviously, a present. Now, the custom among the Chinese is that the recipient of a gift never opens it in the presence of the giver. So I thanked him and went my way. From the shape, the package seemed to be a framed picture of some sort. Had the elder given me a warning, all neatly framed, to take my unwelcome presence out of Chinatown and keep away? As soon as I got around the corner, I tore off the wrapping. The picture was a large photograph of himself and his family.

I began to take heart. Perhaps he wasn't angry, after all.

I ran into another friend, who, thinly disguised, also appeared in the book.

"I've read your book," he said, soberly.

"Yes?" I replied, hesitatingly.

"Are you going to write another?" he asked.

Feeling that I might as well be brave and bluff it out I said, "I think so."

He frowned as he said, "If you do, don't mention me." Then he smiled and added, "Will you, *please?*"

I felt better. But it was time for a showdown.

"Why are all of you so cagey about the book? And do you like it?" I asked, bluntly.

"What do you think?" he asked.

"Damned if I know—and you've got me worried."

He shook his head sadly. "Can't you puzzle it out? Tch! Tch! You've written a book about the Chinese in which you speak of our seeming modesty—and yet you don't know this answer."

It was suddenly clear to me. How could they come out and express an opinion about the book? It concerned them. To admit openly that they liked the book would not have displayed the proper modesty. There were other ways of letting me know. And in time I did find out.

Later, in World War II, one of my Chinese friends wrote me from an army camp, saying, "The joke is on me! I'm taking an orientation course, and in order to make *me* understand the Chinese, I'm having to read *your* book! What are you going to write next?"

The answer to that was, obviously, "more books about the Chinese."

And so it happened that at the ripe age of fifty, when if I had been a businessman or remained a college professor I would have begun to think of retiring—instead I found myself, at long last, able to devote my entire time to writing.

❧❦

14

IT'S SO EASY

There's a friend of mine who always looks down his nose at me in scorn.

"You writers certainly have an easy life," he says.

"Is that so?" I answer, belligerently.

"That's so. And don't give me any arguments. You never punch a time clock. You get up when you feel like it, go to bed at any old hour. Your time is completely your own. You gripe about how hard writing is, but you loaf most of the day. You get to know such interesting people, too, and all your friends spoil and flatter you. Then, when your book is published, you go on the radio, give lectures, autograph books, and have a wonderful time."

"That's what you think," I murmur. "But if you really knew—"

"Don't tell me!" he answers. "It's so easy. All you do is put a sheet of clean white paper into your typewriter—and there you are —a writer."

He's right, there. But that sheet of clean white paper bothers me. I often spend hours just staring at it. But I've heard that for authors living at Mark Twain's old home on Fifth Avenue, writing is no problem at all. His ghost still haunts the place. And tenants simply dust off their typewriters, put in a sheet of paper, and then hurry to the nearest bar to spend the day with other writers, talking about themselves. When they get back home, tired and worn out, lo and behold, the ghost of Mark Twain has written a story for them.

To me, the great paradox in being a writer is that, while I love people, yet when I'm writing about them, like Greta Garbo, "I want to be alone!" And often, when seated at my typewriter, the very people I'm writing about can be an awful pain in the neck.

When I was living on Perry Street I had my typewriter beside the window facing the street. Right in front of our apartment all the children from blocks around had their playground. And just when I started work and tried to concentrate, they'd start yelling and screaming. At first I asked them politely to go somewhere else. I got the Bronx cheer. Then I ceased being polite. I leaned out of the window and yelled at them to get the hell out of there. Again I got the Bronx cheer—a double one.

One sweet little girl had a mirror. She loved to sit in the sun and, just as soon as I would start typing, she'd flash the mirror so that the reflection would hit me straight between the eyes—and out of my mind completely would go my immortal words. When I yelled at her to move on, she and her little friends made faces at me. I asked their mothers if they couldn't do something about it, and have the children play somewhere else.

"What—in front of my house?" one indignant mother asked me. "I have them all day long. It won't hurt you for a few hours. What kind of a man are you, whose heart is not touched by innocent childhood at play?"

I phoned the police. A cop came to see me. I told him how difficult it was to concentrate with a lot of children yelling and screaming at me.

"It's tough," he said, all sympathy. "I understand. I've got six kids myself. Sometimes they make a hell of a racket. But maybe you're the type of man who doesn't like children."

"I love them!" I exclaimed. "I wish I had a dozen of my own. But when I'm trying to write—at that moment I hate the sight of children!"

"What are you writing?" he asked, politely.

"Stories about children," I answered.

"Oh!"

He gave me a peculiar look and walked away. I knew he wasn't going to do a thing about it. He didn't. So I started writing nights, when no one would disturb me. One hot July I was working on a Christmas story. Yes, Christmas stories for magazines are usually written in July, just as Fourth of July stories are written in December. Magazine editors have to plan ahead, and are never seasonable in their thinking. Perhaps that's why magazine editors are peculiar, too.

This hot July night I couldn't get my thoughts straight. So, about one o'clock I went for a walk, to think things over. I sat down upon a stoop in our neighborhood, buried my head in my hands, and groaned aloud. Along came a cop. He gave me a suspicious look. I rose and moved down the street, and sat down upon the steps of another house. The cop followed me.

"What are you doing?" he asked.

"I'm writing a Christmas story about a Chinese child," I replied. "Go away and leave me alone!"

He moved on, but kept looking back over his shoulder. I got up and found yet another stoop.

He came up and said, "Still writing that Christmas story about a Chinese child?"

"Yes." I smiled sweetly. "I'm trying to think how to decorate the

Christmas tree. What do you think would be suitable for a Chinese child?"

"Haven't a thought," he answered.

"Then go away and leave me alone," I snapped.

But he didn't take the hint. "Why don't you write your Christmas story at home?" he asked.

"It's too damn hot at home," I answered. "I'm trying to cool off and imagine what the streets look like around Christmas time, with snow on the sidewalks and holly wreaths and candles burning in the windows. Christmas cheer, you know—good old Christmas cheer, with eggnog and blazing logs in the fireplace. Can't you just see it?"

"What—in July?" he said. "Where do you live?"

"Down the street."

"Sure?"

"Of course I'm sure. Damn it, I should know where I live, shouldn't I? Go away and leave me alone. Just when I'm getting in the mood for writing a Christmas story, you're spoiling it all by talking to me."

"I think you'd better go home," he said. "Come on."

He gave me a helping hand and lifted me to my feet. What could I do but get up? Resist an officer of the law? Hardly.

"You think I'm a liar," I snapped.

"Damned odd, writing a Christmas story in July."

"Come on. I'll prove it to you."

When I got home, I rang the doorbell. I woke up my wife.

"Who's there?" she said sleepily.

"It's me with a policeman," I said.

"Oh, migawd! Wait until I find my dressing gown."

Pale-faced and frightened, she opened the door. When she saw that I really did have a policeman holding me by the arm, she gasped.

But before she could ask, "What have you done now?" I hastily said, "This officer is suspicious of me. Will you please tell him what I'm doing?"

"Oh," she said, smiling brightly. "He's writing a Christmas story about a Chinese child—and why don't you leave him alone?"

The cop looked at my wife, who has a most honest face. He looked at me.

"Well," he said, "I think the place to write Christmas stories in July is in your own home, and not go wandering around the neighborhood. Stay home and write your story."

"It's too late now," I said. "You've spoiled my Christmas mood, and I can't do any more writing tonight. But when the story is published, I'll send you a copy. Got any kids?"

"Yes," he answered. "But they ain't Chinese."

It's things like that which make the writer's life such a bed of thorns. It isn't that we are peculiar. It's just that other people don't understand us.

Even neighbors can be annoying. I have one who likes to play his Victrola as loud as possible. During the summer, when the windows are all open, he turns it on full tilt, and it fairly blasts the roof off. Now, I don't object to music while I'm trying to write. I often put on a record. But I like classical music, something sweet and soothing to get me in the proper mood. My neighbor loves jazz and swing, which irritates me beyond measure.

One morning when my thoughts were flowing very well indeed, he started playing his Victrola. It was the same record, over and over. I began to repeat myself. I went outside and peered into the open window next door. There sat my neighbor, whom I had never seen before, staring vacantly at his typewriter. So he, too, was a writer! I politely told him that if he had to have music while he was writing, it was all right with me, I understood; but would he please not play it so loud? He said he would tone it down, as he, too, understood. Then I asked him if he would also please put on another record, as he had been playing the same record all morning long.

"But I haven't been," he answered. "Every record is a different one."

"They all sound alike to me," I murmured.

The worried look left his brow. He smiled happily. "Thanks! Thanks!" he cried. "I review new recordings for a magazine, and you've said exactly what I want for my opening paragraph. They all sound alike!"

He started pounding the typewriter and paid no more attention to me. I later learned that his name was Barry Ulanov, and that he had written a book on Bing Crosby.

I have other neighbors who aren't writers. Now, they know that I am home all day long. I am not one of those wealthy authors, like Mary Roberts Rinehart, who can afford a soundproof office hidden away in a fireproof building. So I do my work at home. And it never fails: on that wonderful morning when I'm in the mood to write and the words are flowing along easily, the telephone always rings. It's my neighbor upstairs. She had just bought a new chair and expects it to be delivered sometime today. Now she won't be home, and when the chair comes would I please take it into my apartment and keep it until she gets home?

Then the doorbell rings. On the third floor a charming couple have a baby. I answer the door. It's the diaper service for the baby. But mamma isn't home. She has gone for a walk in the park. Would

I please take the diapers? Then there's the Fuller Brush man. Also the friend who calls me on the phone to ask what I'm doing, and when I tell her I'm busy writing, she goes ahead and chats for a full hour. Then there are friends just passing through the neighborhood, who know I'm home and so stop in for a few minutes' chat, and stay, and stay, and stay.

One morning the doorbell rang. When I answered it, there stood my next-door neighbor. She's usually a smartly clad woman, neat and trim. But this morning her hat hung over one ear. Her face had streaks of soot running from cheek to cheek. Her new dress was smudged and torn.

"What's the matter?" I asked, thinking she had gotten into a fight.

"I've been climbing through the coal bin," she sobbed.

"Good lord, why?"

"I took Donald to the train. He's gone to Washington—and he took the keys along with him. Can I come through your apartment and climb over the garden wall?"

"You certainly can!" I answered.

I found a ladder, propped it against the wall, and went back to my typewriter. I desperately wanted to complete a certain paragraph while the thoughts were still fresh in my mind. I looked out the window. There she stood, viewing the ladder with dismay.

"If I climb over that, I'll ruin my nylons," she said.

What would Sir Walter Raleigh have done at that moment? Exactly what I did. I went into the garden, climbed over the wall, jumped down on the other side, and landed sprawling right in the center of her tulip bed. I managed to crawl into her apartment through an open window. When I unlocked the door and let her in, she was all smiles.

"Thank you!" she cried. "Wait a minute until I wash my face and then I'll mix you a cocktail. What are you writing now?"

"I'm not writing this morning," I said. And then, lest she misunderstood, added, "That is—not writing any more this morning."

When she went into the kitchen to fix the cocktails, she saw the tulip bed.

"What's happened to my tulips?" she exclaimed.

A few moments previously I was Sir Walter Raleigh. Now I became George Washington. "I cannot tell a lie," I said. "I fell into the damned bed."

"So I see," she said, frostily. But, being a gracious person, she added, "Well—I'll fix you a cocktail, anyway."

Now I became Sir Galahad. "Thank you," I answered, equally as frosty. "But I never take a drink before five o'clock in the afternoon!"

I went back home to my typewriter. But, worn out physically by my commando tactics and exhausted emotionally by my guilt at having ruined her tulip bed, I could only sit and stare at the sheet of clean white paper in my typewriter.

Now and then, even landladies can stop the flow of words. One summer, during the Prohibition era, I was living in a sublet apartment on the East Side—pretty snooty, right on Park Avenue if you please. I was writing a play at that time. Now, Mae, the superintendent's wife, was not interested in what I was doing. She had her own business. Every now and then, butlers would drive up in limousines and deposit laundry baskets with Mae. She must have had quite a neat little income on the side for doing this special sort of laundry.

One morning she rapped on my door. "I've brought you a little drink," she said. It was a very fine whisky sour.

"Thanks," I murmured, and laid it on the table.

"Go ahead—drink it," she urged.

"Later," I said, "when I have finished my morning's work."

"Oh, go on—now. It won't hurt you."

The only way to get rid of Mae was to drink the whisky sour, which I promptly did.

"How does it taste?" she asked.

"Fine!" I answered.

She smiled happily, and said as she vanished, "I'll be back shortly."

In an hour, came a rap on my door. It was Mae again. I was in the midst of an important scene, but what could I do? Perhaps Mae had another whisky sour for me. But she hadn't.

"How do you feel?" she asked.

"Fine!" I answered.

"No headache?"

"No."

"Got pains in the stomach?"

"No!"

"Got dizzy spots before the eyes?"

"No! I'm fine—thanks!"

"Good," exclaimed Mae. "Then I guess it's all right."

"What's all right?" I asked.

"The whisky," she said, and then explained. "You've seen a lot of chauffeurs bringing me laundry baskets. Well—it ain't laundry. My husband gets a lot of choice Scotch from a friend he has on a boat. Last week that friend got caught. Somebody squealed on him. Pat has more orders than he can handle, so he had to go to a bootlegger himself. I wasn't sure whether or not it was really good stuff. We got some high-grade customers—and they'd be sore if they got poisoned. So I thought I'd try this case on you. You didn't have a headache, no stomach-ache, no blind spots—so I know it's okay—and now we can go ahead and sell it!"

All that summer Mae would bring me drinks, and then wait to see the result. I might add that the play I was writing never sold.

Of course, suffering as I do with all these varied and sundry interruptions, I should know better than ever to interrupt some-one else. But once the temptation was too strong. Now, there are probably more writers to the square inch in New York than in any other city in the United States, even Los Angeles. The subways, the busses, the bars are crowded with novelists, short-story writers, and playwrights. All you have to do is stop a stranger on the street and ask, "How's your second act?" and you'll get an answer.

One hot summer day I was strolling through Greenwich Village, where typewriters click like mad, day and night. Before an open window, pounding a typewriter like hell-bent-for-election and in the hot throes of creative endeavor, was a very lush-looking young woman.

I said, "How's your second act?"

She paused a moment, gave me a quick once-over, saw my gray hairs, my stooping shoulders, my thin legs, and said, "A damn sight better than your first!"

She slammed down the window and went right on typing as if nothing had happened. Maybe it's just that I'm in need of a psychiatrist to straighten out my complex on being interrupted. But I do know that the greatest problem I've ever had to face along this line came from my father-in-law.

Now, Herb was a most distinguished, aristocratic gentleman of the old school. Whatever ideas he had concerning morality, man-ners, and politics had been formed at an early age, and he never changed his opinions. He had lived many years in Philadelphia, where as he always said, "It was a privilege and an honor to be a Democrat!" He was the only man, outside of the Communists, whom I have ever met who knew exactly how to vote and never faltered. Whenever he'd go to the polls, Herb would vote the straight Democratic ticket, regardless of who was running for office.

I don't know if this is a trait in common with other conservative Democrats, but Herb never read a book. Certainly he never read one of my books. But there was a reason for that. He didn't like me or approve of me as his son-in-law. Whenever I'd show Herb a book I had just had published, he'd give it a supercilious glance, and say, "Hm—well, it's got nice illustrations."

But once he did read a book, from cover to cover—every word, in fact. During one of the recent campaigns a Republican friend of ours sent us a copy of John T. Flynn's *Country Squire in the White House.* Now, Herb admired Franklin D. Roosevelt above all other men. He had pictures of him plastered all over his room—and Herb was convinced that no harm could come to the world or himself while Roosevelt ruled in the White House. So I politely handed Herb the copy of the book.

"You may enjoy this," I said.

When he saw what it was about, he replied, "Well, I'll most certainly read *that* book!"

And he did—every word. When he finished it, he said by way of comment, "I sort of got the impression that that writer didn't like Roosevelt any too well."

But Herb did read the *New York Times* most religiously. He'd take the sport section with him to the bathroom in the morning, and sit there from half to three-quarters of an hour. Then, after lunch, he'd read the paper line by line and word by word. After dinner, he'd pick up the *Times* and reread it all over again.

If he didn't get his paper every morning, or by some chance got a copy of the *Herald-Tribune* instead, Herb would be in a temper. That summer when there was a newspaper strike—and no *Times* —both Sue and I wondered how we could cope with the situation. The first two days of the strike were unbearable for us. Then I solved the problem. Every night I got a certain newspaper and handed it to Herb in the morning.

It was his habit on a summer evening to take a chair into the garden and there read the paper until night fell. He always wore his hat, too. So, during the strike it was a most enjoyable sight for the neighbors and ourselves to see dignified, conservative Herb, seated in the garden with his hat on, reading the *Daily Worker*.

When the strike was over, I asked Herb if he wanted me to continue to get him the *Daily Worker* or did he want to go back to the *Times?*

"I like the *Times* better," he said. "It's got more news."

Herb was really quite justified in his disapproval of me as a son-in-law. Writers are difficult persons to live with, anyway, and especially if they are around the house all day, as I was—and as Herb was, too. Sue, before we were married, had a career of her own, and kept at it even after we were married. So she was always at work during the day, while I sat around the house, clad in pajamas and bathrobe. This was something Herb never understood. In his day and generation, men always went to work mornings, properly dressed, while the women stayed home.

And I must confess, too, that I get up in the morning when I feel like it. Sometimes it's eight o'clock—although not too often.

Usually it's around nine. But there have been times when, due to circumstances beyond my control, I haven't gotten up until noon. Now Herb, rain or shine, was always out of his bed every morning at six o'clock. Just why, I never could puzzle out, for he had nothing to do all day but feed the cat, read the *Times*, and water the garden.

Once, in the cool of an evening when he was reading his paper, our neighbor on the left turned on the hose, and Herb got sprinkled. This made him angry, and I think he was justified. But instead of speaking politely to this neighbor, he decided to have his revenge in his own way. So the next morning he turned the hose into the neighbor's garden. But he got the wrong garden. He sprinkled the washing on the line in the garden to the right. My telephone began to buzz, and the irate neighbor wanted to know what, why, and wherefore!

I left my typewriter and dashed into the garden, and told Herb.

"You're sprinkling the wrong garden," I said, hoping he would see the error of his way.

"Is that so?" he said.

The next morning he again sprinkled the garden, and this time turned the hose both to the right and to the left. I had two angry phone calls.

At this time it happened that I was writing books about the Chinese, and extolling their love and respect for their elders. I was practically drooling about the beauties of old age, and how wonderful it was to be old, and how remarkable were the Chinese elders whom I knew. But then I'd have Herb suddenly burst into my room and ask, "What have you done with my pliers?"

"I haven't touched your pliers," I'd answer. "What would I be doing with your pliers?"

I'd leave my typewriter and go help him find the pliers, which

were inevitably right where he had left them. Then I'd return
to my typewriter, and go on expressing—or trying to—my beautiful sentiments about the glories of old age.

On the last New Year's Eve that Herb was with us, he said he
wanted to make a toast.

Lifting his glass, he said to Sue and me, "Here's good luck and
happiness to you both."

And that's the way I like to remember Herb, a gallant gentleman
of the old school, even though he was a little out of step with the
present day.

≫≪

15

YOUR LITTLE BOOK

I HAD just had a book published. It had a bright and colorful jacket; strong, durable binding; good, readable print; and some very excellent illustrations. Then my publishers phoned, saying that they had arranged for me to be interviewed over the air by that well-known lady commentator—let's call her Mamie Kluckhorn.

I had never been interviewed over the air, and so I asked timidly, "What—what do I do?"

"Nothing—nothing at all," was the blithe answer. "She'll ask you questions about your book—and you give the answers. That's all. She has millions of listeners, and they all read books. Don't be nervous."

It was as simple as that, and I was thrilled. Having once been an actor, I would now become a star of the radio just like Boris Karloff, Frank Sinatra, Franklin P. Adams, and others. I mailed post cards to my friends, advising them of the great event and asking that they listen in and later tell me what they thought.

I certainly felt grateful to my publishers. They were doing a fine promotion job on the book, in arranging for me to appear on Mamie Kluckhorn's program. They had also sent her, at their expense, two copies of the book, so that she would know what she was talking about.

Came the day. According to instructions, I arrived at the marble halls of the radio station fifteen minutes before the appointed time. Finally I found a uniformed guard, who ushered me with great pomp into the studio where the broadcast was to be held. Seated at a table was a young woman making some notes on a manuscript.

"Miss Kluckhorn?" I asked.

Without even glancing up, the young woman said, "No. I'm Glutz—her secretary. Who are you?"

"I—well—I'm supposed to be interviewed—"

"Oh—you're the one. Sit down. Don't be nervous. Mamie will put you at your ease."

I sat down. I really was nervous, thinking of the millions who would hear me this morning. And Miss Glutz's statement didn't have the soothing effect she probably intended. Soon after this, a bored young man strolled in, adjusted his tie, and gave me a suspicious look.

"I'm supposed to be interviewed," I said, apologetically.

"Oh, yeah? Relax. No need to be nervous."

My blood pressure went even higher. For a fleeting minute I wished I were safe at home; but then, I had told my friends about the broadcast, and, after all—there were millions of listeners who bought and read books.

Silence. Then Mamie Kluckhorn, in all her glory, burst into the studio. She was young and amazingly beautiful, and had all the freshness and enthusiasm of a retarded spring morning.

"Hi, Glutz! Hi, Pete," she gurgled.

I now identified the bored young man. He was Pete, the jovial announcer who soothingly joked with Mamie now and then and gave her his moral support when she ran out of words—which wasn't often.

"How do you like my new hat, Pete?" she asked.

"Neat number!" he replied.

"Make some crack about it. May get us a new sponsor."

Mamie slapped on some fresh lipstick, saying, "Yum-yum." She grabbed the notes from Glutz, sat down in front of the microphone, and then gave me the once-over.

"You're the guest star," she said sweetly. "You wrote a book. I liked it. Hope you write another. Now let's test your voice. Say something."

"Something," I murmured.

A voice from nowhere boomed out, "That's fine. Tell him to get a little closer."

"Speak into this," suggested Pete, indicating the microphone.

"Talk to me just like you would talk to your wife—and don't get nervous," said Mamie.

I started to make a reply, but Pete, his finger on his lips, silenced me by whispering, "Sh! We're on the air."

Suddenly, most informally, Mamie began speaking. "Hello, folks, of the listening audience," she said. "This is your old friend Mamie Kluckhorn speaking, and back again this morning for a half hour of fun and information. I had a wonderful time last night at the fascinating fashion show held at the Waldorf Ball Room, and I saw the most fascinating—"

She made a frantic gesture to Pete, who, quickly taking the hint, said, "Hat! Isn't that a new hat you're wearing this morning?"

"It certainly is, Pete. How observing you are," giggled Mamie. And Pete laughed, too, just as if it really were a very funny joke.

For the next five minutes Mamie described in detail all the latest styles she had seen at the fashion show, while I, in a cold sweat, waited for my hour to come.

Finally Mamie seemed to remember something she had completely forgotten. With an air of great surprise she turned to me, and said, "And today we have a most interesting guest here in the studio, a man who has written a truly fascinating book, a real bestseller." (This was news to me, but I didn't contradict her.) "And he's going to tell us all about his exciting and thrilling book. But before he does, I want to say something about a new product just on the market. It's Julia's Magic Facial Cream, comes in gift packages, which—" And on Mamie went for another five minutes.

Eventually she remembered me again and, smiling blithely, said, "But to come back to Carl's new book. Tell me, did you enjoy writing this book?"

My thoughts were in a turmoil. I didn't know what to say. Had I enjoyed writing the book? Damned if I really knew. All I could remember were the two years of work, of agony, of indecision, of interruptions, of hope, anguish, glory, and despair that had gone into the writing.

Pete waved at me frantically to say something, and all I could do was murmur, "Why—yes—you see—I—"

But Mamie saved the day for me. "I thought so," she beamed. "Everybody enjoys writing books. It's a lot of fun. Some publishers have told me I should write a book. What do you think, Pete?"

Pete in his smooth, well-modulated baritone voice answered glibly, "I certainly do, Mamie, especially if you say something in your book about Mamma's New Baking Powder."

Mamie, in a feigned shocked voice, answered just as glibly, "But I can't do that, Pete. They're one of my sponsors, and what would they think?"

Whereupon both Pete and Mamie laughed heartily, as if that were truly a wonderful joke.

"However," Mamie went on. "Let me tell you something about Mamma's New Baking Powder. It's all the advertising says it is, and—"

When she had finished telling her millions of listeners all about the baking powder, she came back to me. "That's a perfectly wonderful story you tell, Carl, on page—" she grabbed frantically at the notes Miss Glutz had handed her—"yes—on page 462. Do tell us about it."

I gasped. Page 462? It couldn't be. There were only 327 pages in the whole book. I wiped the perspiration from my brow, and said meekly, "What story?"

But again Mamie graciously came to my rescue. "But before Carl tells us the story, I want to say something about Dizzy Soap Suds, which certainly will solve the problem about what to do with Junior's jumpers when he soils them by playing in sand piles."

Glancing at the clock, I saw that there were only five minutes left. But Mamie consumed them by chatting gaily about her beloved suds.

But she hadn't forgotten me, for in conclusion she said, "Wonderful having you as our guest today, Carl, and I know my radio listeners have enjoyed hearing all about your new book.—This is Mamie Kluckhorn saying good-by until tomorrow morning, when I'll be back on the air again at this same time with another interesting guest author who has written a truly fascinating book."

The interview was over. Mamie rose, smiled at me, and said, "Sorry—have to run along. I'm having lunch with Ilka Chase. Stop in my office, please, and autograph your books. Sign one to my dear mother. She likes to read, too. By-by, by-by."

She blew a kiss to Pete and was gone. Still in a daze, I followed

Miss Glutz into a cubbyhole of an office. Glutz thrust two books at me, which I promptly autographed, saying, "Yours gratefully." Then I glanced at the jackets and turned pale. I had autographed copies of a book called *Ferment in Europe*, or some such title, by a well-known foreign correspondent.

"But this isn't my book!" I said to Glutz.

"Doesn't matter," she replied. "Mamie sends all these books to hospitals and orphanages, anyway. When you write another book, let us know, and we'll have you on the air again. Good-by. Nice knowing you."

But that was my farewell appearance on Mamie Kluckhorn's magic hour. In due course of time, I wrote another book, and was again invited to go on the air with other lady commentators. None of them was like Mamie. In fact, I have reasons to believe that some of them had actually read my book. And certainly there have been some who have most graciously allowed me to talk, and have asked me most intelligent questions about my books, even though these comments were sandwiched in between praise of the various products they got paid for sponsoring.

When my book on the Chinese, *Three Times I Bow*, was published, one well-known commentator, chatting with me before the program, asked, "Tell me, do the Chinese have cockroaches in Chinatown?"

"I presume so," I answered. "They're found pretty much all over New York, it seems to me."

"But haven't the Chinese some typical Chinese way of getting rid of them?"

"I don't know," I replied truthfully. "Why do you ask?"

"Well, I thought it would be wonderful if they did. I've a new sponsor, a marvelous cockroach powder, and I was hoping I could tie it up with your book in some way."

Of course, as time went on and I had more books published, I made more appearances on the radio. And while I have never gotten over being nervous, still I have thoroughly enjoyed being interviewed by such charming and gracious ladies as Mary Margaret McBride, Alma Dettinger, and Nancy Craig.

But there was one other lady with whom I got so nervous that I made an awful ass of myself. Before the radio program I had given her not only a short autobiographical sketch, which she wanted for her introductory remarks, but also a short statement of the point I wished to make in this particular book.

We sat facing each other, as is customary, with the microphone on the table before us. The commentator had, as usual, a handful of assorted notes on her products and a list of the questions she was going to ask me. I had nothing but a few scattered thoughts in my head. I was again urged not to be nervous. Then, after the customary opening comments and a few plugs from the commentator about the health-giving qualities of Philadelphia Scrapple, I saw by the gleam in her eye that my turn was coming.

"We have as our guest today—" she said, and then began to fumble with her notes. It was obvious that she had forgotten my name and couldn't find my biographical sketch. But she wasn't daunted as she continued her search. "Yes—a most interesting author—who is—"

I came to her rescue. "The name is Carl Glick," I said humbly.

"Oh, yes—and he's written a book—" And again she fumbled for the notes. They scattered all over the table, and a few sheets of paper fell to the floor. She couldn't remember the name of the book either, and I felt that the questions she was going to ask me were now on the floor out of reach.

But the announcer jumped into the breach. I had talked with him before the program and had told him what the main point of my comments was to be. He had a quick memory. He mentioned the name of the book, and then went right on to tell the things I was planning to say. When he had finished he turned to me and said, "Isn't that so?"

I suppose I should have responded simply, "Yes." But I didn't. I knew that if I didn't say something right away and keep on talking, I'd not be able to say another word on that broadcast. And I thought, too, that if I went on talking, that would give the commentator time to find her notes and rearrange them. So on I went —and while the commentator stared at me, I gave what amounted to a monologue. I talked solidly, without stopping. But I kept one eye on the clock, and as the second hand crept around to the last closing seconds, I thanked the commentator for the privilege of being on her program, and shut up.

She had just time to say, "This is ―――― speaking, and I'll be on the air again tomorrow morning."

She continued to glare at me. Then she gathered up her notes, and said frostily, "This is the first time in my experience I haven't been able to mention my sponsors!"

I left the studio in disgrace, and I've never been asked to appear on her program again. Thank God!

Now just why, because a man has written a book, he is also expected to be a brilliant public speaker is something I have never understood. But, immediately upon publication of a successful book, all the women's clubs swoop down and want the author to appear before them in person, and make a speech. Usually for free, too. Perhaps they like to look at writers. Perhaps they think that if they hear the author tell about his book, they won't have to read it. The general feeling among publishers is that if the ladies see and hear an author, they'll immediately rush out and buy his little book. How wrong they are, particularly in my case. Now, my books have bright jackets, but personally I'm sort of moth-eaten. And it has taken me quite some time to reach the conclusion that authors like myself should be read and not seen.

There are some few of us who are very handsome, but not many. The majority are either too thin or too fat, and get such a bad attack of stage fright that we mumble and can't be heard beyond the third row. When I give a talk and my books are on display, some middle-aged matron always picks up a copy of one of my books, looks it over carefully, glances at me, and then says, "What a good-looking book!"

A writer like myself should have a double, a handsome young lad with wavy hair and a lush smile. Let him give the speech, while I pose as his secretary, and sit in the back and enjoy myself. And I'm reasonably certain that if the good ladies of the women's clubs heard a young Apollo with broad shoulders talking about a book, they'd not only buy it and read it, but feel just as highly stimulated mentally as they do in the movies watching Clark Gable make love.

Giving talks before a woman's club invariably follows one pattern. Upon arrival in town, you are met by the reception committee and driven about town to see the historic spots.

"This is where Edgar Allan Poe's mother is buried," I am told.

I have to murmur, just as if I cared, "I didn't know she was buried here."

"Oh, yes. I thought you would be interested. Poe was a writer, too, you know."

There's no proper reply to that, so I ask politely, "Do you have many writers speak to your club?"

"Oh, yes. One every month—if we can get them."

Wondering whom I would be competing with, I always ask, "Whom did you have last month?"

"I've forgotten his name. But he was most stimulating, and told us all about his experiences as a deep-sea diver. He had lantern slides, too." Then comes a great smile of anticipation. "But next month we're going to have John Mason Brown!"

Then I am driven to the auditorium and thrust into a dark and dismal anteroom to await the arrival of the members of the club and their guests. Finally, I am ushered upon the stage, together with the president of the club and the good matron who is going to introduce me. If I could only start speaking right now, all might be well. But no—while my nervousness increases momentarily, I have to sit and face a sea of faces and bobbing hats, while the business meeting is being conducted. The minutes of the last meeting are read and approved. New business comes up and is tabled. The treasurer's report is read, penny by penny and item by item. It, too, is approved as read. Then announcements of local forthcoming events are made from the floor. Everybody is urged to attend the church supper, which is for the purpose of raising money to buy a new organ. Then someone makes the suggestion that, instead of a speaker at the last meeting of the year, they have a flower show. That, too, is approved. My heart thumps a bit, as I begin to suspect that perhaps after all the good ladies don't particularly like speakers—with or without slides. Then the lady who is to introduce me is introduced.

Now, she has been selected because her grandfather was once a missionary to China, and this afternoon I am going to talk about the books I have written on the Chinese. My introducer has prepared a speech of her own. She now delivers it. She tells all about Grandfather, and how he dearly loved the Chinese people and actually converted ever so many of the heathens. Then she says that, since my travels in China, I have written a book, and that now I am going to tell them all about my experiences, and that she knows it is going to prove to be most stimulating, as missionaries to China always have so much to tell.

I stagger to my feet. I apologize for the misinformation about myself. I say I have never been to China. I have only been to China-town, and my books are about the Chinese in America. Then I add that I have never been a missionary and that I haven't even attempted to convert a single one of my Chinese friends. This doesn't go over too well, and I can see the church workers sort of stiffen and frown in disapproval. But I struggle and stammer on, and finally I have said all I have to say. But now comes the question period. A lady with a funny-looking hat and a stern expression rises and asks me what I honestly and truthfully think of Madame Chiang Kai-shek.

How can I answer that? I've never met Madame Chiang. I admit this, to the disappointment of my audience, who now, I feel, are quite convinced I don't know what I'm talking about. But the lecture is over—and I long for a drink. I get one. But it's tea. So for the next half hour, balancing a tea cup in one hand and a plate with a lone sandwich in the other, I chat informally with the ladies, and a few of them tell me that someday they hope to read one of my books.

Once, however, a white-haired, charming dowager said to me, "I did so much enjoy reading your book."

That made me very happy, and I thanked her and meant it.

"Yes," she gurgled on. "I particularly liked your book *The Good Earth*."

Before I could make a reply, another dowager standing beside her said, "Aren't you confusing him with Frank Buck, who wrote *Bring 'Em Home Alive?*"

The first dowager looked at me as if I had thoroughly deceived her and she didn't like that at all. "Perhaps I am," she said haughtily, but, not to be discourteous, added, "My grandchildren are very fond of animals. Perhaps some day you'll take them to the zoo and tell them about your experiences."

"I'd love to," I murmured.

When I could, I made my exit and hurried alone to the nearest bar.

Then there was the time I was privileged to give a talk from the pulpit in a church. I was to be paid a set sum for it, too. I thought a collection had been taken at the door as the audience came in. But no!

When I had finished my talk, the pastor stood up and said that the ushers would now pass the plates, and there would be a freewill offering. The organist began to play *America*. The audience rose and started singing. I stood up, too, facing them. Up and down the aisles went the ushers, passing the plate. My mind wasn't on our national hymn. I was wondering how much would there be in the collection plates, $5.42 or $3.86? Here at last was the ultimate test of whether or not my so-called talk was worth anything, or whether I should pay the audience for the privilege of speaking. So there I stood until the last thin penny was collected, more nervous and ill at ease than I have ever been while delivering a lecture.

"I trust it came out all right," I asked the pastor afterwards.

"I think so," he responded politely. And to this day I don't know how much was taken in or what my talk really was worth.

But there's one compensation in writing a book. You do, because of the book, meet people and make new friends. They are all so curious about a writer. Busybodies? I'm just an old reactionary by comparison. There was one charming lady of indefinite years who phoned me, wanting to know if I was the Carl Glick who wrote *Shake Hands With the Dragon?*

I confessed to my guilt. Without even asking if she were welcome, she said, "I'm coming right over. I want your autograph in the book." And she hung up the receiver before I could tell her that I was busy.

The doorbell rang, and there she was, the book in her hand. Now, it's always flattering to have someone ask you to autograph your book. And I couldn't be impolite and not let her in. So in she bounced, thrust the book at me, and said, "Say something cute!"

Now, how in hell can you say something cute to a stranger? It would be easier to write another book. So, for the moment, I laid the book aside. I thought I would ask her a few questions about herself, if I could manage it adroitly. But did I get a chance? No, she started asking me questions about myself.

"Do you have regular writing hours?" she asked.

"Yes—from nine to two! And every day."

It was now twelve o'clock, but did she take the hint? She did not.

"Do you know what you're going to say when you start writing, or do you find out what you're saying after you have written it? Do you write on the typewriter directly, or do you write in longhand first on a pad and then retype? Do you find certain hours are better than other hours for writing? When do you think best? And where is it you do your writing?"

I showed her my desk and my typewriter.

"Oh," she said, "it's a portable."

Then she began to snoop around the room. She asked me what every object was, and where it came from. She even opened the closet door and counted my two suits. She peered under the beds.

"What are you looking for?" I asked.

"Your unsold manuscripts. Where do you keep them?"

She fired questions at me faster than I could answer them. Finally, it got to the point that I was even more curious than she was.

"Why are you asking me all these things?" I said.

She calmed down for a moment. "Well," she replied. "You see— it's this way. I want to know just how a writer lives. What he does that is the thing to do, and what he does that isn't the thing to do. Oh, I have a purpose in asking these questions. I want to know for myself. I want to know if I'm doing the right thing or not. You see —I've decided to be a writer, too!"

Now the only proper reply to that was to ask, "What are you writing?"

"It's my first book," she answered modestly. "I don't know whether I should tell you or not. It's still a secret."

"Most writers are like that," I answered. "They don't like to talk about their books. So if you don't want to tell me—"

"Oh, but I do," she said, and paused and looked coy, as if she expected a little coaxing.

"Well, what is it?"

"My autobiography!" she answered.

"Wonderful!" I murmured.

"Yes—I've met so many interesting people and had such exciting experiences, I just feel I must tell the whole world about them."

"Good luck!"

"What are you writing now?" she asked.

I needed no coaxing to tell her. "My autobiography," I said.

"But that's my idea," she stormed.

"The hell it is!" I answered rudely. "It's everybody's idea."

Then I thought of something to say in the book she wanted inscribed. So I wrote, "Success to your autobiography. May it be suppressed!"

"That's perfectly wonderful," she said. "If it only would be!"

There's another thing about writers that arouses curiosity, and that is how much money an author makes. I'm always being asked.

One of my uncles once asked me how much I received for a short story. I told him, and then asked him what his yearly income amounted to.

"Carl," said my aunt sternly. "That's not a polite question."

"Why not?" I answered. "If he wants to know what I make, why shouldn't I ask what he makes?"

"But he's interested. Everybody is curious about writers. And it's wonderful to know that you can write a little story or a book and actually get paid for it!"

16

❧

STORIES I'LL NEVER WRITE

Some years ago I was strolling along 51st Street west of Fifth Avenue. The old brownstone houses here were standing bleak and empty, waiting for the wreckers to tear them down to make room for Rockefeller Center. Along came a well-dressed woman, swinging in her hand an empty champagne bottle.

When she got in front of one of the houses, she paused, broke the bottle on the steps, and said lustily, "To hell with you!" Then she thumbed her nose at the house.

Sensing a possible story, I asked her, "Why did you do that?"

"I lived there once!" she replied, giving me a supercilious grin.

"You must have been very happy there," I suggested.

"Happy—in that dump?" And again she thumbed her nose at the house. "Had I been, I wouldn't have launched it on its way out with an empty champagne bottle."

"I bet there's quite a story in why you did this."

"There's a story!"

I was all set to have it, so I pulled my favorite line, "I'm a writer."

She gave me a cold stare. "You expect me to tell you—of all people—a writer—what went on in that house when I lived there? To hell with you, too!"

She thumbed her nose at me, and stalked away. There must have been a good story here—but I didn't get it.

Then there was another house and a mysterious little old lady who lived there. The house was on East 4th Street, just off the Bowery. Once upon a time, around one hundred years ago, this had been one of the fashionable residential districts of New York. But with the passing of the years, the wealthy and the fashionable had moved away. Their old homes had been torn down and loft buildings erected. Now the neighborhood had a shabby, down-at-the-heels appearance. But in the middle of the block one old home remained. Despite the surroundings, it still held its head high and proudly. The iron-wrought railings on the steps were kept in fine repair. The brass on the door knobs was shined and sparkling, and the sidewalks in front of the house looked as if they had been swept every morning. However, all the windows of the house were closed and shuttered save the windows on the second floor.

Evenings, as I would walk along 4th Street on my way to the Church of All Nations, where I was leader of the Chinese Athletic Club, I would pass the house. Leaning from the second-story window was a little, white-haired old lady. She would be looking up and down the street as if she expected someone to appear around the corner. I took to waving to her as I'd pass by. She'd smile and raise a hand in greeting. I often wondered who she was, and why, at this hour in the evening, she would always be looking out of the window. Later in the evening and during the day she wouldn't be there.

Then one evening the window was closed, and on the door hung a wreath of flowers. I knew that the little old lady had passed away. And I felt that I had lost a friend.

I searched the newspapers and finally found a brief mention of the death of Miss Gertrude Tredwell at her family home on East 4th Street at the age of 93. She had been born in 1840. That meant that she had been a young woman at the time of the Civil War. I wondered about her. Had her lover gone off to battle and not come back? Had he promised to return at a certain hour in the evening? Was that why she was always there at the window at that time, looking up and down the street, waiting and hoping he would appear?

Only recently I was again walking along East 4th Street. The old house has been restored by the Historic Landmark Society, and, known as "The Old Merchant's House," is now open to visitors. I went in and was shown around. The mystery deepened even more. I was told by the guide that, during the last years of her life, Miss Tredwell had closed the entire house save the two front rooms on the second floor, where she lived with a companion. She had been born in this room, and here she had died. After her death trunks of dresses of the Civil War period had been found in the attic. There was one of white, which might well have been a bridal gown. It had never been worn. There were other dresses, partly finished and then packed away. I was also shown a trap door that opened onto a secret hiding place in the second floor and led, so the guide told me, to an underground passage into the garden at the back. Nobody knows today just what this was for.

There are on display, besides the gowns, shell combs, bright ribbons, and gay trinkets—all the feminine finery so dear to a young girl's heart—that have been stored away for more than fifty years. Old newspapers were also found, with accounts of events during the Civil War.

What was the secret passage for? Why were the gowns never

finished? Why were some of them never even worn? And what was the story of the little old lady who waved so gaily to me, a stranger, night after night as I passed along the street?

Then there was another mysterious person whom I never met, either. I never even knew what he looked like. This was during the time I was at San Antonio. We took one of our plays to a small town on the Gulf of Mexico. The hotel where we stayed overnight, the only hotel in town, was a run-down, shabby place, and the proprietress was a grim-faced, solemn woman who might have been the mistress of a buccaneer.

My room was on a court, facing another wing of the hotel. But I had a sleepless night. In a room directly across from me the lights were on full-blaze. Here, seated with his back to me, fully clothed and wearing a cap, I saw a man. Nothing very unusual in that. But the way he sat was unusual. He didn't move. There he sat, silent and motionless as death. I pulled down my shade, but the light still bothered me. I got up again and looked across the court. He was still sitting silently in the same position. This began to bother me. But what could I do about it? I finally, however, fell asleep.

The next morning, when I looked out of the window the lights were off and the man was gone. I went around the corridor and found the room number.

When I went down to breakfast, I asked the proprietress what that man was doing in that room last night.

"What man?" she asked suspiciously.

I told her what I had seen.

"There was no man in that room last night!" she said, and shut up, silent as a clam.

I was glad to get out of the hotel and back to sunny San Antonio.

Human nature, outside of novels and works of fiction, is often
hard to understand. There were two puzzling dowagers in a little
theater I was directing. They enjoyed coming to the theater
workshop and sewing on costumes. And, day after day, they'd appear in the afternoon, arm in arm, and calling each other "dear" all
over the place. They'd go back to the sewing room and start work.
In less than half an hour I would be summoned.

Mrs. Blank had moved into a dressing room all by her lonesome.

She'd say to me, firmly but distinctly, "Please go ask Mrs. Doe
to return my scissors."

I'd hurry to Mrs. Doe, who would sputter and fume, and say,
"What am I doing with her old scissors? Please ask her to return
my needles she borrowed."

I'd get the needles. The ladies had quarreled, obviously, and
weren't speaking. I'd groan and decide I'd have to find two other
good workers to help with the costumes. But at the end of a wearing day and in time for tea, the two ladies would emerge from their
hiding places. They'd glare at each other a moment, and then, arm
in arm, march out of the theater, calling each other "dear" and
"darling"—just as they had when they stormed into the theater.
Evidently all was forgiven.

But the next day they'd be back again at the theater, and the
same performance would go on. I never did learn what it was all
about, and why they invariably quarreled when they started sewing.

This is a story with two heroes, something no writer should
ever attempt. One of the heroes is Siegfried, immortalized in song

and story, the hero who in Richard Wagner's opera knows no fear. The other is Sam Angioletti, an eleven-year-old Italian boy, quite unknown to fame. But Sam wasn't afraid, either.

I met Sam when I was working at the Church of All Nations, back around 1933. One of my assignments was acting as a sort of counselor to the Vikings, a boys' club. Sam was one of the members of this club.

He lived over on the lower East Side, where the streets are narrow and noisy, the tenements dark and crowded, often with more than one family living together in a small three-room flat. There are no trees on the street, and no grass in the back courts. The only bit of green to be found is, here and there on the fire escapes, a forlorn plant with faded, wilted leaves. In those days there were speakeasies and junk shops, pushcarts with fruit and vegetables that uptown stores had discarded the day before yesterday, dirt, squalor, and poverty—and all day and all night, the thunder of the Elevated. Not a very pleasant place to live, that East Side.

But Sam didn't seem to mind, for this background was all he had ever known. He was a bright, talkative youngster. Sam was in business for himself. He claimed that he gave the best shine on the East Side for only five cents. Early every morning he started out with his shoe-shining box under his arm, and he hurried about until late in the afternoon. Some days he made as much as fifty or sixty cents. There wasn't as much business on the streets now as formerly, for there was unemployment and poverty on the East Side during the Depression, and the derelicts on the Bowery didn't bother about well-kept shoes. However, Sam had a few steady customers in the speakeasies, and often their tips were generous. Sam bought all his own clothes, and there were times when his day's earnings went toward the family dinner.

For recreation, Sam played about the streets in the evening, and occasionally, when feeling prosperous, went to a ten-cent movie, where he saw gangland in all its Hollywood glamor. Once a week he went to the Church of All Nations to play games for an hour and have a swim. That day was the best in Sam's whole week.

Now and then, after the club meeting, the boys would ask me to tell them a story. It didn't take me long to discover that Sam and his pals didn't care much for "Goldilocks and the Three Bears." Nor did they like gangster stories either. Perhaps they saw enough of that sort of thing in their everyday life. Anyway one day, hard pressed for a story, I told them about Siegfried as Wagner had dramatized him in the opera. I managed to make it a sort of continued story, for after all no one can tell the entire plot of *The Ring* in ten minutes. There was something in the adventures of Siegfried that seized upon Sam's imagination. He couldn't wait until the next week to learn what happened to Siegfried after he killed the dragon; so, meeting me on the street, he offered me a free shine if he could hear the rest of the story. I accepted his proposition.

The next week there were some boys present who hadn't heard the beginning, and I asked Sam to tell them the story.

"This here Siegfried was a swell guy," said Sam. "He wasn't afraid of nothing, so one day Mime says to him, 'You're afraid to forge the sword,' and Siegfried says, 'No, I ain't,' so he forged the sword. Then Mime says, 'You're afraid to kill the dragon,' and Siegfried says, 'No, I ain't,' and so he killed the dragon. Then because he wasn't afraid and had killed the dragon, he was able to hear the boids sing, and the boids said, 'Mime is a crook, a dirty double-crosser, and he's after your dough, and you're afraid to kill him,' and Siegfried says, 'No, I ain't,' so he killed Mime. Then he heard the boids again, and they says, 'There's a beautiful goil waiting to be rescued and she's surrounded by fire,' and Siegfried wasn't afraid of the fire nor the goil, either, so he rescued her. He was some guy, this Siegfried."

The Valkyries also appealed to Sam. This is the way he explained these warrior maidens. "They's women that go around doing good, like the women at the Settlement. But they ride on horseback and rescue soldiers that get killed. Then they take them to heaven, where they give 'em all they want to eat and drink and show 'em a swell time."

When I told Sam that the story had been set to music, he was even more interested. I invited Sam and some of his friends to come over some afternoon to hear some recordings I had. I was a trifle dubious as to just how Sam would respond to the music of the Ring on a first hearing, for there have been some Park Avenue dowagers who have found it hard going. But one afternoon Sam and some of his pals came over to the apartment. They were attired in their Sunday best, which meant clean shirts and neckties. Sam's little face was scrubbed and his hair slicked back, and plenty of soap had removed the stains of the shoe polish from his hands.

"Now, you guys sit back and shut up," said Sam to his friends. "We're going to listen to some music, and you like it—see!"

The first record I played was the "Forging Song."

"You can hear the anvil and everything," said Sam. "And that one that sings so squeaky is Mime, ain't it? I don't like that guy. He's a crook."

The music of the "Forest Murmurs" Sam thought was "swell." "You can hear the trees and everything," he said. "That's just what I imagine it's like in the woods. Quiet, and you don't hear nothing but nice sounds."

When it came to the scene between Wotan and Siegfried, Sam wanted to discover for himself the dramatic moment where Siegfried, who wasn't afraid of anything, breaks the spear of Wotan, who tries to bar his path. When the great, crashing, descending chords burst forth, Sam sat up and said, "He's done it. Gee! That's swell. Just like I imagined."

Sam was excited and happy. Forgotten was the East Side. Forgotten was the shoe-shining box, the pounding of the Elevated, and the hard knocks of the life Sam knew. Of all the motifs of the opera, Sam loved best the "Hero Motif."

"That's exactly what a guy who ain't afraid should sing," he said. "It's a good one to whistle on days when business is bad."

When World War II came, Sam, then a grown young man, enlisted in the Marines. I was told that on the beachhead at Okinawa, Sam came face to face with the dragon—but I am certain he was not afraid.

17

IRFAN WANTS A WIFE

IRFAN's home is in a small village in Bengal, India. But he had been in New York but a few weeks when he decided he'd like to get married, settle down, and live here for the rest of his life. He was thrilled by the novelty of the city, and would stand for hours gazing at the skyscrapers, getting a great deal of amusement out of the strange behavior of the natives. I wouldn't have known about this if I hadn't been a busybody.

You see, ours is a quiet neighborhood in an out-of-the-way corner of Greenwich Village. Nothing much ever happens in this part of town. Now and then a husband beats his wife, but only when she deserves it. And occasionally a drunk, stumbling home, gets into the wrong apartment and spends a pleasant, restful week end. I know of one man who remained two years. Ultimately he married the girl.

So when, during the last war, over one hundred Indian seamen appeared, we were all intrigued and interested. A bit of old India had arrived in New York. They were Moslems, I was told, and had been rescued from the British boats torpedoed by German submarines. They were quartered at the Seamen's Y.M.C.A. over on the water front, a few blocks from where I live.

It was quite a sight, really, seeing them walk single file along our peaceful streets in the approved jungle fashion, led by an elderly man. He was the advance guard, keen-eyed and quick to give the warning should a wild Greenwich Villager attack from the bushes, as tigers are apt to do in Bengal. The rest followed in order of their social position—based on age and their importance in the villages back home. They wore ill-fitting cast-off clothes that had been given them after their rescue. Some had bright-colored sashes about their waists. Others let their shirts hang outside their trousers.

Not many spoke English, and those who did knew only a word or two, so they had their difficulties in the stores in the neighborhood. But they made their wants known by pointing. They bought scissors, knives, and needles and thread. They liked incense, too, and over at the Jackson Square Pharmacy they sampled all the sweet-smelling hair ointments and shaving lotions until they found their particular choice—rose water. They bought every bottle the drugstore had—and asked for more.

One day I was in a restaurant around the corner, having a glass of milk, when six of them strolled in. They stood and shyly observed what every person at the counter was having. One, a trifle bolder than the rest, saw my glass, came up, nodded, and smiled.

"Milk," I said.

He pointed at the glass, then at himself, and repeated the same performance with the others. His meaning was clear. I passed on their order to the waiter, and soon they were all seated in a row at the counter.

"Speak English?" I asked.

"Me speak," said the spokesman, grimly and soberly. He was a dark-skinned youth, bright-eyed, with finely cut features.

The ice being broken, I said, "Hello?"

He responded with something which sounded to me like, "Bala ah-sue me, bun do?"

I might be saying the wrong thing, but I repeated it to the others. To a man, they rose, bowed, and said, "Salaam! Salaam!" They began chattering, pleased and excited that someone had spoken to them in their own tongue. I later learned that what I had said was "hello" in Hindustani, and that translated it means, "You are good, I hope, my friend?"

Having finished their milk, they laid down some money on the counter and were very surprised when the waiter gave them change. Later I was to find out that they thought the United States was a wonderful country—a man gets paid here for buying something!

They followed me out onto the street. We stood on the corner, looking at each other. There wasn't much I could say, but I said it, "Salaam! Bala ah-sue me, bun do?"

Bowing and smiling, they echoed my sentiments. It was a lot of fun, conversing with them. All I could do was to repeat myself, however—which I did several times, and always got the same answer.

What English the spokesman knew was only a few simple words. He wasn't able to form sentences. Yet we managed to understand each other.

He asked me, "Wife?"

"Yes," I nodded.

"Many?"

"One."

He looked very sad as he replied, "Bad—bad." Then he pointed to himself, and said, "Me three wife."

I congratulated him by saying, "Salaam! Bala ah-sue me, bun do?"

"Salaam!" he answered.

Then he indicated each of the others in turn, saying, "He four wife—he two wife," and so on. Each time I bowed, smiled, and said my little speech. They responded politely in the same manner.

When the spokesman explained to them that I had only one wife, they all shook their heads sadly. I felt somewhat ashamed of myself, and tried to apologize by telling them that the American custom allowed but one wife to each man.

"America rule one wife bad!" he said.

The next question he asked me was, "Live?"

I pointed down the street, and said, "There."

So off we went. I led the way. They followed in single file. This made some of my neighbors laugh.

When we got to the front door, I paused. For several weeks now they had been passing along our street, seeing the doors and the curtained windows and probably wondering what went on inside the houses and what sort of lives the Americans lived behind those walls. Had I been in India, I would have been just as curious about them and would have given my eye teeth to be invited into an Indian home.

"Come in," I said.

So in they trooped.

"Sit," I said.

"You sit," my English-speaking friend replied.

Later I discovered that, because I was the elder, politeness demanded that I sit first. I sat. They sat. They stared politely. It was the first time they had ever been inside an American home. One leaned over and felt the rug. Another fingered the upholstery on the chair. They were puzzled at the pictures on the walls.

"Come—look!" I said.

And they did. The feature attraction was the icebox. I showed

them how it worked, and the ice cubes. Someday I'd like to go to
Bengal, where these men came from, to sell refrigerators. I'm certain
I'd find no sales resistance whatsoever. Finally, their curiosity satis-
fied, they left.

"Salaam!" I said. "Come see again."

"Salaam! We come!"

And they did, in twos, threes, and singly—at seven in the morning, at eleven in the evening, at any odd hour they pleased. Always
they brought along with them some new visitor who had to see an
American icebox with his own eyes.

"Sit!" I'd say.

"We sit," would be the reply. And then we'd sit and look at each
other until I started conversation by saying, "Salaam. Bala ah-sue
me, bun do?"

"Salaam!" they'd reply, and that would go on for five minutes.

Finally they brought around one of their number who spoke
quite a bit of English, and I learned their story. He told me that
they had signed aboard British boats in Calcutta. Some had come
from villages one day, two days away from that port. Others were
city bred, and several were college boys. In all, they weren't much
different, really, from a group of our own boys stranded somewhere
in a foreign land.

One of them told me that his boat had been torpedoed off the
coast of South America. The English captain and crew were taken
aboard the German submarine. The Indian seamen were put adrift
in boats. Then the ship was sunk. For twenty days in the lifeboat
they fought the wind and the sun. Some of the older men died at
sea.

"Finally friendly ship come up," he said. "Me taken on board.
I so weak I no stand. But safe—and so I was born again."

I asked him where he lived in India, and showed him a map. He placed his finger on a spot in northern India. Then he closed his eyes and was silent. There was a look of infinite sadness on his face. For a long time he was silent. Then he opened his eyes, looked up, and smiled.

These seamen received from the British Government for spending money, so I was told, only two dollars a week. The pay due them was held back until such time as they went to sea again. Yet, such being the custom, when paying a visit they always brought a present of something to eat—a package of cookies, an orange, a loaf of bread. I would give them coffee or tea, but best of all they liked a glass of cold milk from the magic icebox. Since I was the elder, they insisted on serving me first. Their good manners were quite overwhelming.

One day they asked me to visit them at their quarters in the Seamen's Y.M.C.A. They had a huge dormitory on the top floor, crowded with row after row of cots. There was only one chair, and since I was the guest, it was dusted off for me to sit upon. They all had taken off their ill-fitting American coats and trousers and wore white linen dungarees with *dhotis*—bright-colored cloths—wrapped around their waists. Barefooted, they sat cross-legged upon the cots, smiled, and said, "Salaam." And so we conversed merrily as usual.

Leaving, I saw in the hall a row of them kneeling on their prayer rugs, facing east. These Indian seamen making the Mohammedan devotions in one of our Christian Y's was as pleasant a sight as I've seen in many a day.

There are only some three thousand Indians—exclusive of these stranded seamen—living in this country at present. They are mostly merchants, but there is a colony of farmers in California. The others are students, teachers, and writers. Often, because of their dark color (though the Indians belong to our Caucasian race), while traveling in the South they are mistaken for Negroes and treated as such. So, below the Mason and Dixon line the Indian women always wear native dress and the men put on turbans.

Among those I knew, there was one who came to see me oftener than the rest, always bringing a gift of food purchased out of his two dollars. He didn't speak a word of English. He'd sit quietly for an hour or so, rise, bow, and go his way. One day he paid me a special visit, bringing with him the interpreter. I offered them a glass of beer.

The interpreter told me that Moslems do not touch intoxicating liquor, as it is written, "Let not the first drop pass your lips." But Irfan—that was my guest's name—was a smart man. He took the glass of beer, dipped his finger in, flicked the first drop upon the floor, and, obeying the letter of the law, drank the beer.

Then after the usual "Bala ah-sue me, bun do?" the interpreter said, "Irfan is no friend."

I wondered what I had done wrong. Obviously something. But the interpreter explained.

"You older than Irfan," he said. "He younger. Only men same age say 'friend.' You elder—so Irfan says you his American father —he your Indian son."

I was told that henceforth the correct thing to do was to address him as son, and he would reply, "Ah-me bala ah-sue, baba," meaning, "I am very well, father."

I said I was flattered and honored to have Irfan adopt me as his American father. He was forty-nine, and since I was fifty-three, I felt pretty good about it.

That Irfan had a scheme up his sleeve never once dawned on me.

Having heard my speech accepting Irfan as my son, they went their way. But the next morning, bright and early, they were back. At seven o'clock the doorbell rang. I wanted another hour's sleep, at least. But I admitted my son and his interpreter.

"You sit," I said, indicating chairs in the living room.

"We sit."

"You sleep," I then suggested.

"We sleep!"

Immediately they both closed their eyes. I went back to bed for another hour's rest. When my wife came into the living room, she received quite a jolt, finding two Indian seamen sound asleep. But they never opened their eyes or made a murmur until I got up at my usual hour. Then they had breakfast with me, and only after that did the interpreter get down to business.

He said, "You American father—Irfan, Indian son. India rule is that father always gets wife for son. So you get wife for Irfan."

"Salaam!" I said.

"Irfan say he no want go back boat. No like boat. No like British. Irfan say America good. Irfan like America. He stay here in America, get wife, get job, work here rest of his life until he get tired. He stay America with wife and no go back British boat."

The interpreter continued, "India rule is that wife bring husband two thousand rupees. You find wife with two thousand rupees for Irfan, he start business and become American citizen. Irfan married before. He good husband. Very good man."

They sat, waiting for my reply. There was no doubt of Irfan's years of wisdom, experience, and charms. Yet I wondered how many American women would be willing to pay two thousand rupees for a really good husband.

The interpreter explained further. "India rule is also wife come and spend month with Irfan. If at end of month Irfan no like wife, she go back home."

"Does Irfan keep the two thousand rupees?" I asked.

The interpreter chatted a bit with Irfan, who nodded in the affirmative. Now, my understanding of the Indian custom is that the husband, under these circumstances, returns the dowry. But Irfan had been here long enough to have ideas of his own about American big business. If he didn't like the first wife I found for him—and my guess would be, he wouldn't—it would then be up to me to find another. In time, I could see Irfan as a very rich and much experimentally married man.

I told Irfan I would find out what could be done about it. And I did try. I asked several unmarried women that I knew if they had two thousand rupees and would like an Indian husband, with myself as their father-in-law. But they all told me that if they had two thousand rupees, they'd rather purchase a new fur coat, or a vacuum cleaner, or take a trip to Florida in the winter. So I did not meet with success. I have always felt unhappy about it, for I am afraid that my son did not consider me a worthy father.

Just where Irfan is today, I do not know. One morning he and his interpreter came to see me, and I was told, "Irfan go E-lease Eye-lan."

I think he meant Ellis Island. I asked, "Why?"

I was told, "Irfan no like boat. No go back British boat. British say no go boat, go E-lease Eye-lan. Irfan go and sit."

It wasn't long after that that Irfan stopped coming to see me. For a time there was a canteen in the neighborhood for these seamen, conducted by friends of India. But the British Government closed it down, and opened a canteen of its own uptown. The seamen I

knew were moved to quarters near-by. And we didn't see them
in our part of town again.

We miss them, for they were friendly and polite, and it was a
pleasant sight to see these men of India walking our streets and observing for themselves, at first hand, freedom in a democracy. I
often wonder what they really thought of us. I wonder, too, where
Irfan is now. Is he back home again in his native village in Bengal?
Has he one wife—two wife—three wife—and did he get his two
thousand rupees?

18

※

IT'S THIS WAY

I WASN'T feeling well that particular morning. When Sue saw me, she seemed worried.

"You look terrible," she said anxiously. "What's the matter?"

"I haven't slept for three nights," I answered.

"Conscience bothering you again?"

"No. This time it's writer's insomnia."

I was in one of those periods when I didn't know what to write about next.

But I don't think Sue really believed me, for she suggested, "Perhaps you'd better consult a psychiatrist."

"I don't need a psychiatrist," I sputtered. "I know what's wrong with me—even if I have been acting peculiarly lately."

"Then you'd better see your doctor."

So, taking her advice, which as usual was all to the good, I made an appointment with my doctor. When I arrived at his office, he held a small pad in his hand, which he consulted from time to time. He made me open my mouth, stick out my tongue, and say, "Ah!" He took my blood pressure. He thumped me on the chest. Then he hit my knee with a little hammer.

Shaking his head dubiously, he said, "Now what do *you* think is wrong with you, this time? And where do you ache the most?"

"I don't have an ache," I answered. "I just don't sleep nights."

"Why not?"

"It's those damned ghosts—they keep me awake."

He looked puzzled and glanced at the pad in his hand. "Just relax. Do these ghosts make you talk to yourself?"

I was so tired from lack of sleep that I was growing more nervous and irritable by the moment. "I don't talk to myself," I muttered, belligerently. "What makes you say that?"

But I felt I knew the answer. Sue had probably phoned him and told him all my symptoms.

"Whom do you talk to, then?" he asked gently. And, glancing at his pad again, he added, "Who is Slaughter-house Mary? You had better tell me everything."

So I told him. I explained how, after getting in bed and listening for a time to the relaxing "Music to Read By" on the radio, I am all prepared for a good night's rest. But then the ghosts begin to appear. They come trooping in through the windows. They pop out from behind chairs and tables. They crawl out of the mantelpiece. They sit and look at me. Some grin at me lovingly, some scowl maliciously; but, angry or happy, they all look at me hopefully—and wait for me to do something about it.

"Do you recognize these ghosts?" asked the doctor.

I nodded. "One is Slaughter-house Mary, whose name you have there."

"Who's she?"

"A lady wrestler I met once. Then there's the Countess, too. But she really wasn't a Countess at all."

"What was she, then?" he asked, growing more patient and gentle with me momentarily.

"She was a former artist's model. But when she got too old to pose in the nude, she called herself a Countess and tried to sell oil stocks to millionaires."

"Are these the only two you recognize?" he asked.

"No," I answered. "I know them all."

"Who are they?" He seemed determined to get at the truth.

"They're the countless people I've met from time to time, about whom I've thought someday I'd write a story. Some of these ghosts I love. I'll write nice, friendly stories about them. Other ghosts I loathe. I'll make them my villains. But there they are—just when I'm trying to get to sleep. And I lie awake thinking about them and talking to them, and wondering whether, if I really did write a story about them, I'd have the truth. That's why I can't sleep nights. It's nothing but writer's insomnia. It's an occupational disease."

By this time I was so angry at his standing there so damn patiently that I snapped, "And what are you going to do about it?"

"You should take a trip to Bermuda and relax!" he said.

"I can't afford to go to Bermuda. I'm a writer!"

"What you need is a rest," he advised.

So off he bundled me to a hospital. I took along a suitcase filled with mystery stories. I'd forget my own, for the time, and see what the other fellow was doing. I was fully prepared to catch up on my sleep and have a nice, easy, restful few days, doing nothing at all.

But the first morning, just as I was becoming absorbed in an exciting mystery, into my room popped a plump, nicely groomed nurse.

"I've come to take your temperature," she snapped.

"I haven't a fever," I replied. "I'm here for a rest. I'm a writer."

"I've come to take your temperature!"

She thrust a thermometer into my mouth, took away my book, felt my pulse, and wrote down comments on a chart. Then out she bounced. I went back to the mystery. An hour later, in bounded another energetic nurse.

"I've come to take your temperature!" she said.

I started to protest, but in vain. I had my temperature taken again.

"Find anything wrong?" I asked.

"You're not supposed to talk," she said. "It only excites you!" Then she left the room.

Half an hour later, there appeared a third nurse, a veritable amazon of a woman. She was carrying a sponge and a basin of water.

"All right," I said. "Take my temperature and to hell with it!"

"I'm not going to take your temperature. I'm going to give you a bath."

Now, happily I had a room with a bath, so I said, "Not necessary. I've already taken a bath this morning. I'm a writer!"

She glared at me and said, "I have orders to give you a bath."

She threw back the cover of my bed.

"Go away!" I yelled. "Why should you give me a bath? I'm perfectly capable—"

But by that time she had ripped off my pajama tops and was dousing me with cold water. I yelled some more. But again it was in vain.

"Stop tickling me!" I said. "I'm a writer!"

"I'm not tickling you. It's your imagination!" she replied. "Now just relax. Take it easy. Don't get nervous. We are all your friends here."

"I doubt it!" I exclaimed.

She tried to be patient with me and made no reply. I fought her for a moment or two, but she overpowered me and gave me my bath. When she had finished, she told me to put on my pajamas, and then straightened the bedclothes.

"Now, don't you feel better? More relaxed?" she said.

"No!" I groaned. "How many times a day do you bathe me?"

She gave me a haughty stare and left the room. Far from being relaxed, my nerves were in a worse state than ever. What would happen in the next hour? I grabbed the telephone and called the doctor. I told him what was going on, and asked if I had to submit to more torture? Were they getting ready to put me into a strait jacket?

"Just relax!" he said. "I'll find out and phone you right back."

He did, too, saying tenderly, "Take things easy and relax. It's all a mistake. They got you mixed up with the patient in the next room. He's really violent."

But I wasn't bothered again, and after four restful days in the hospital I went back to work. I felt most grateful to the doctor. His advice was good. I looked upon him as a friend, and decided I'd write a story about him some day. Now he's another ghost that haunts me nights.

Often he stands there waving his unpaid bill and saying sweetly, "Just relax." I take his advice, and do.

Being a writer makes it possible for me to know other writers. How we all love each other. Once I was at a swanky literary tea, where writers of all sizes and descriptions were thicker than rejection slips on our unsold manuscripts. Everybody was talking about himself and lying like mad about the number of copies his latest book had sold.

One portly, well known male foreign correspondent was holding forth to a starry-eyed young poetess, who looked at him adoringly and in open-mouthed wonder.

"I've had a most remarkable career," boomed the foreign correspondent, in his best lecture voice. "I've been shot at in Africa. I was stabbed in Siam—but recovered. My enemies tried to poison me in India."

"Yes, oh yes," gurgled the poetess. "I can well understand. I've read your stories, too."

When our books are published, we often exchange autographed copies, saying such kindly and well-meant cheering words as, "To X, with love, may your latest book sell a million copies, too."

Once I even went so far as to buy a copy of a friend's book, and took it around for him to sign. He was very pleased and happy as he autographed it for me.

"You're lucky to have a copy of this book," he said. "It's rare now —out of print."

"Yes, I know," I said. "That's why I bought it."

"Where did you get it?" he asked.

"At a second-hand book store, for ten cents," I replied truthfully.

I pass him on the street every so often. He nods briefly and hurries on his way back to his typewriter.

Once I wanted a first printing of one of my books for a faithful nonliterary friend. The only place to find one, I knew, would be in a second-hand book store. So I rambled into one. But, being modest, I couldn't tell the book dealer what I was looking for.

"Got any first editions of Zola today?" I asked.

Now, first editions of Zola are hard to find, too. But the dealer didn't have any. So I browsed about a bit. And, sure enough—

there on his shelves was the first printing of my book that I wanted.

"What do you want for this silly little book?" I asked.

"Oh—that! You can have it for a quarter. Quite a comedown from Zola!"

There's one vice common among my writer friends which I don't possess. I do not read aloud either my unpublished or published manuscripts. You see, I'm a coward, and afraid that I'll be told the truth.

Once I attended a writers' conference, and I broke all records. I was the only practicing as well as beginning writer present who didn't read aloud a single line from anything he had ever written. One reason was that I didn't have any manuscripts with me.

There was one well-known novelist attending the conference who was in charge of the seminar for the novel. After telling the students all about the thirty-six possible dramatic situations and explaining in detail how and why he wrote his novels, he ran out of things to say. He could only read aloud from one of his novels, which he did —and was so overcome as he read his favorite passages that tears flowed down his cheeks. Everyone was quite thrilled. It was a wonderful experience for the student writers.

Two days later, at his usual session he read aloud again. Again tears flowed. But nobody much cared this time. He had forgotten what he had read the first time—and so read the same passages all over again.

However, with beginning writers it's quite another story. They should be encouraged. And if they hear their stories read aloud by someone else, they might possibly learn quite a bit.

I remember one charming elderly lady who had written her first play. She spent the entire winter inviting friends in for dinner. When they had been wined and dined properly, she read aloud her play, from cover to cover. When she had finished, she always asked for suggestions. But nobody dared give her any. How could they, after drinking up all her liquor and being worn out after a three-hour reading session?

And, as one of her best friends so aptly put it, "Even if May's play is produced, I don't know who will come to see it. Everybody in New York already has heard it read!"

Still and all, *I* firmly believe that young writers should be encouraged and helped whenever possible. And I'm only too glad to sit for hours, telling them just how I write myself. I'll even read aloud a few pages of my latest book, to show what I mean and prove my point. And if they don't want to listen, they can go elsewhere— and to hell with them!

The reason for this writer's vanity is simple. Take the actor, for example. When the curtain falls on the last act, the audience—his public—applauds. And the actor knows that they have enjoyed his performance. The same is true of the musician at a concert. And even painters, having an exhibition of their work, see the public standing around and admiring. But consider the poor author. He hasn't a chance to sit and look at people reading his book. Does anybody really read it? The writer doesn't know—unless he gets a fan letter.

I'm a dope when it comes to fan letters. I love them. I don't care even if I get a letter from a stranger tearing me limb from limb. If he hadn't actually read the book, he wouldn't have bothered to write me. That's a triumph of sorts. But when I get a letter from someone telling me that they have read my book and liked it—I'm in seventh heaven, and impossible to live with for the next few days.

"What are you writing now?" a friend asked me, not so long ago.

I told him about this present book, and even offered to read aloud a few chapters. He was very polite about it, but said he'd rather wait until the book was published, and then he could read it all.

Then he said, "I do hope that you'll state strongly some place how you feel about the important problems of the day."

He's very young and inclined to lean toward the left politically. When I told him I doubted that I would do as he suggested, he asked me, "Why not? The world is in such a turmoil today that you should take a definite stand on pertinent issues."

I answered him firmly. "Look—I'm fifty-eight. I no longer feel strongly on any subject but one. The world has always been in a turmoil—and probably always will be. Why should I say anything to add to the confusion? Often the headaches of today are the jokes of tomorrow. Political parties come and go. Even governments rise and fall. And, after all, it doesn't matter too much under what form of government a nation lives—there'll always be people. Rich and poor, fat and thin, young and old. They'll love and hate, weep and laugh, struggle and fail, hope and succeed, live and die. And no matter what happens in this world, there'll still be people with stories worth writing about.

"That's why I have fun being a busybody," I said. "And I'm going to continue to be a busybody—for I hope to meet and know more people—and perhaps get a story now and then. To me the most fun in this world is knowing all the exciting and crazy people in it.—You see, I'm a writer—"

He was thoughtful a moment, then he said, "You know, there's something that happened to me once—"